"I've learned more about in[...] son than from anyone else [...] through his timely treatment of topics such as AI and remote work. I can only imagine the difference it would make in the church and in our world to see Christians catch and implement this vision for their work."

—Collin Hansen, vice president of content, The Gospel Coalition; author of *Timothy Keller: His Spiritual and Intellectual Formation*

"In *Why Your Work Matters*, Tom Nelson encourages and challenges readers to cultivate a 'hopeful realism' in their approach to work. Though we live in a broken world, Tom emboldens readers to work with and for God, detailing inspiring stories of whole-life transformation and renewed identity in Christ. This book is a helpful guide for those seeking to commit their work to the Lord and honor him in their callings and career paths."

—Robin C. John, founding member and chief executive officer, Eventide

"In *Why Your Work Matters*, Tom Nelson provides an eminently readable overview of the why, where, and how of work. If you judge a book by its relevance to your life and its ability to bring you closer to knowing God, then you'll be hard-pressed to find a better book from the past five years."

—Henry Kaestner, cofounder of Faith Driven Movements, Sovereign's Capital, and Bandwidth

"Tom is one of the great shepherds of our age. He possesses the unique skill of writing with the pen of a pastor and the heart of an entrepreneur. His passion is to awaken a vision within us driven by the truth that our work matters. Every page echoes with words of ancient wisdom and powerful affirmation that your work matters to you and your community, that it's a praise to God. *Why Your Work Matters* removes the fog, allowing us to see clearly God's plan for using us to shape and share his story of redemption."

—**Chris Brooks**, senior pastor, Woodside Bible Church; host of *Equipped with Chris Brooks*

"Dallas Willard said that our work is our primary place of discipleship. How could that truth not cause us to take a more reflective look at the work we do? As well, the landscape and future of work looks very different. Tom Nelson's work helps us sit with these issues and consider deeply how to reorient ourselves to God's story about our vocation. Sit with these pages. You and the world will be better for it."

—**Nancy Ortberg**, chief executive officer, Transforming the Bay with Christ

Why Your Work Matters

Why Your Work Matters

how God uses our everyday vocations to *transform* us, our neighbors, and the world

Tom Nelson

Brazos Press

a division of Baker Publishing Group
Grand Rapids, Michigan

Published by Brazos Press
a division of Baker Publishing Group
Grand Rapids, Michigan
BrazosPress.com

Printed in the United States of America

Library of Congress Cataloging-in-Publication Data
Names: Nelson, Tom, 1956– author.
Title: Why your work matters : how God uses our everyday vocations to transform us, our neighbors, and the world / Tom Nelson.
Description: Grand Rapids, Michigan : Brazos Press, a division of Baker Publishing Group, [2025] | Includes bibliographical references.
Identifiers: LCCN 2024039020 | ISBN 9781587436475 (paper) | ISBN 9781587436611 (casebound) | ISBN 9781493449606 (ebook)
Subjects: LCSH: Work—Religious aspects—Christianity. | Bible—Quotations.
Classification: LCC BT738.5 .N57 2025 | DDC 261.8/5—dc23/eng/20240925
LC record available at https://lccn.loc.gov/2024039020

Cover design by Studio Gearbox

The author is represented by the literary agency of A Drop of Ink, LLC.

Baker Publishing Group publications use paper produced from sustainable forestry practices and postconsumer waste whenever possible.

25   26   27   28   29   30   31   7   6   5   4   3   2   1

To Dallas Willard,

whose brilliant mind, kind heart,
warm friendship, and wise mentoring has
been a treasured gift of grace
in my life and work

Contents

Introduction

We are storied people. From our earliest days, we are drawn to stories. They frame our relationships and animate our lives with wonder, memory, and meaning. They fuel our imaginations, and the stories we hear and tell ourselves shape our daily work.

What story is shaping your daily work? Is it a story of frustration or fulfillment? Is it one of exhaustion or rest, anxiety or peace, meaning or meaninglessness? How is your work going? Perhaps you like your work (perhaps you like it too much). Or maybe you don't, and your work doesn't seem to matter much. Your work may feel invisible and devalued by others. It may leave you feeling exhausted and overwhelmed. You long for the weekend.

It could be that you feel stuck and frustrated, longing for better or different work. It may be robbing you of sleep as you face hard personnel decisions and difficult colleagues. Maybe you are struggling to find a healthy work-life balance. Perhaps you're on the edge of burnout, working hard and not seeing fruitful results. At present you may be unemployed. Do you wake up each morning feeling lost, wondering who you are and where you belong in the world? Are there longings in you that your current story of work is not fulfilling? Does it seem as if you are working in a fog?

1

It was on a curvy stretch of California's picturesque Pacific Coast Highway that we made a quick stop during our drive in the rental car. Our family vacation guidebook had piqued our interest with a story about the rugged shoreline of the Point Arguello area. The day was bright and sunny. A light ocean breeze greeted us as we stepped out of the car. The view of the Pacific Ocean was simply stunning.

As we breathed in the beauty of the moment, my mind drifted to a tragic event that occurred on these shores on September 8, 1923. A squadron of US destroyers steamed southward along the California coast. Led by the USS *Delphy*, the squadron was on a twenty-four-hour training mission from San Francisco to San Diego. Just north of Point Arguello, a thick blanket of fog rolled in. Unaware of the danger that lurked in the fog directly ahead of them, the navigator on the USS *Delphy* directed the column of ships to pivot a few degrees east. Relying on the skill of his navigator, Captain R. A. Dawes cruised through the fog. Suddenly, the *Delphy* smashed broadside into the rocky Point Arguello shoreline. The force of the collision split the hull of the *Delphy* in half. Before Captain Dawes could notify the rest of the squadron, six other destroyers had run aground, their once-impressive hulls lying bruised and battered, listing in the pounding waves. On that fateful, foggy day off California's rocky coast, the United States not only lost some very fine sailors, but the Navy lost more combat ships than they had during all of World War I.

As I stood overlooking the Pacific, reflecting on this naval tragedy, I was reminded of how perilous a blanket of literal or metaphorical fog can be. It is all too easy to find ourselves fogged in when it comes to those things that matter a great deal in our lives, including our work. Of course, we have good intentions. We do not intend to run aground on the many rocky shorelines we inevitably encounter, yet we often cruise through life in a fog, at breakneck speed, without the necessary navigational wisdom. While an unimaginable amount of information is just a click away on the internet, acquiring wisdom is anything but instant. Wisdom requires intentionality, quiet reflection, and a life geared to a slower and more deliberate pace.

When it comes to the story of your work, perhaps you feel as if you're navigating a dense fog at the moment. Is it possible your work needs a new story?

Several years ago I found myself in a thick fog as I struggled to understand my work's importance while navigating my Monday world. As a follower of Jesus of Nazareth whose work is to assist others in their spiritual growth, I have repeatedly run aground on some pretty rocky shores. With the best of intentions and sincerity of heart, I have led others aground on some faulty ideas about how our faith story informs our work story. I have wrongly viewed some kinds of work as being more important than others. On several occasions in my life, I have drifted to the perilous edge of workaholism, conveniently making an idol out of my work. For way too long, I did not see work as an essential component of what people of the Christian faith refer to as "calling." And I did not see how my Christian faith and its story of work could transform my relationships and priorities. I failed to grasp that a primary responsibility of my pastoral work was to assist and equip others to better connect the confessions of their Sunday faith with the practices of their Monday world. I regret that I gave little attention to what people do with the majority of their time. In essence, I was committing pastoral malpractice. Truth be told, my story of work needed a lot of work.

The Christian faith can be understood as a comprehensive and coherent story that speaks into every nook and cranny of human life. For Christians, the Bible is the greatest storybook, one that speaks into the past, the present, and the future. Its ancient writings not only tell an amazing story but also welcome us into it. I believe the Bible gives the most coherent and meaningful story of work imaginable. Yet when it comes to work, many who embrace Christian faith experience a large Sunday-to-Monday gap in their thinking and living. Many Christians tend to embrace the faith on Sunday but pretty much live as if it is irrelevant on Monday. I am using the word "Monday" metaphorically, knowing that many of our work schedules include evenings and weekends and don't always begin

3

anew on Monday. The metaphor of Monday also helps contrast the work we do and times of Sabbath rest and gathering for corporate worship, which is often on Sunday. It is easy for people of faith to say, "Thank God it's Friday," but the Christian story of work should also prompt us to say, "Thank God it's Monday." Our work matters more than we may realize.

I don't know where you are in life or in your faith journey, but I do believe if you are like me, you need a new story that gives you greater confidence that your work matters. A story that brings coherence to your Monday world, a story that is unsurpassable in its meaning, fulfillment, purpose, and joy. A story where living an increasingly integral life now and for all eternity awaits you.

It has been more than a decade since the publication of my book *Work Matters*. I am humbled and grateful that this book has blessed many. Yet so much has changed in the world and in the world of work that needs more thoughtful reflection. A highly disruptive pandemic took the lives of many, shut down economies, and radically changed work patterns. Much work moved online, and many workplaces moved from offices to homes. Remote jobs became the norm and continues to structure much of our work today. We experience increasing stress and exhaustion and greater mental health concerns. For many businesses and organizations, greater challenges have emerged concerning supply-chain bottlenecks, labor supply, and inflation. A pandemic also had a positive effect on the way many of us understand a work-life balance, encouraging us to confront overwork, address workaholism, and explore shorter workweeks that make more time for relational connection and rest.

We are experiencing increasing secularization and politicization, which are influencing workplace attitudes, values, and relationships. A greater emphasis on diversity, equity, and inclusion has emerged. And the dizzying change of technology is rapidly altering the very nature of human work. The rise of artificial intelligence (AI) continues to reshape human work in ways we never imagined, increasing productivity but also job dislocation and loss. AI and similar technologies bring unintended consequences and new dangers regarding privacy, control, and the abuse of power. The world of work feels as if it has been turned upside down, inside out. The one constant we can count on is change.

Much has also changed in my thinking about work since the publication of *Work Matters*. I now understand work as not only what we do in our individual callings but also what we do together in bringing goodness and beauty to the world and adding value for others. One of the primary ways we love our neighbors both local and global is in and through the work we do each and every day. The importance of Sabbath rest has gained greater resonance in my mind and heart as both a posture and lifestyle of the truly flourishing worker. New insights from the disciplines of neuroscience and interpersonal neurobiology shape how we see and experience our Monday worlds. As such, in this new edition, I have added some additional wisdom I have gained as a result of being immersed in, and having a voice in, the broader faith and work conversation. My hope is that this book will be more helpful to you as a result.

In the pages that follow, my heart for you is that you will encounter both a window and a mirror: a window into God's big work story and a mirror to see how you beautifully fit into that story.

In part 1, I offer a look through the window of God's story of work. I highlight his good original design for work and how that design has gone awry in our lives and our workplaces. I explore the very real difficulties of our work and ponder what it can actually be in the world. I focus attention on how God has and is restoring his good design for our work. I even reflect on the hopeful eternal picture the Bible paints of our work's transcendent significance. Imagine the difference it would make if what you and I do every day mattered for all eternity. And I explore how Jesus of Nazareth embodied the importance of work and what the New Testament writers said about it.

In part 2, I offer a look in a mirror, focusing on how Christian faith shapes our lives in and through our work. What would it look like if our Sunday faith connected seamlessly to our Monday work? What are the important implications, challenges, and opportunities that our work provides for us and for our world as we seek to live out a faithful Christian presence in our workplaces?

We all need a new story of work, one that allows us to clearly see past the fog we may be encountering in our Mondays. My hope is that as we go on this journey together, you will more fully embrace the ancient work story of the Christian faith, realizing how much you matter and how much your work matters.

Part 1

God's Story

1

Why Work?

All vocations are intended by God to manifest his love in the world.

—Thomas Merton[1]

The most important questions we ask are *why* questions. As such, author Simon Sinek reminds us to start everything we do by first asking why. "By *why* I mean what is your purpose, cause or belief? *Why* does your company exist? *Why* do you get out of bed every morning? And *why* should anyone care?"[2] The big why questions around who we are and what we do are ultimately answered by the story that frames and animates our lives. As it pertains to your daily work, you might ask, Why do I get out of bed on Monday morning? Why do I work? Why should I (or anyone else for that matter) really care?

I have good news for you. God's story gives a hopeful and life-giving answer to the big why question of work. This story can transform your Monday world. God's story reveals that work is his idea. Actually, God designed you with work in mind. God cares about you and your work, and he desires to be there for you in the midst of it. To get a better grasp of God's design for work, we begin by recognizing that not only did God create us for work but God himself is a worker.

God at Work

In the very first verse of the Bible, God's story of work begins: "In the beginning God created the heavens and the earth" (Gen. 1:1). This signals the importance of work and reveals something important about God himself. God could have initially revealed himself in Scripture in any number of ways, but he chose to reveal himself first as a worker, a creator of the heavens and earth. What does this tell us? That doing good work flows from the nature and character of God. Our Creator God is the ultimate worker and the ultimate ruler with power and authority over all material and non-material reality. The ancient psalmist praises the Creator God's work as one of sovereign dominion—that is, exercising oversight over the entirety of creation: "Your kingdom is an everlasting kingdom, and Your dominion endures throughout all generations" (Ps. 145:13 NASB).

Why did God bring material creation into existence? Why did this all-powerful, all-knowing, all-wise being create us and the universe as we know it? What was God's big purpose animating his work? What was it that in essence "got him out of bed in the morning"? God's big why is truly beyond our limited grasp; however, we can be confident that at least a part of his big why is love. God works because he is loving. The Bible tells us that "God is love" (1 John 4:8, 16). Christian writer and philosopher Dallas Willard helps us see love as more than a mere abstraction but rather as an active expression in the world. He says, "Love means to go out in creative goodness."[3] It is God's love that activates him to unleash his creative goodness in his creation masterpiece. God's work story is a grand love story.

A Work of Love

One of the most unforgettable experiences is the birth of a child. Holding an infant in our arms is a marvel beyond words. Observing their beautifully crafted tiny fingers and toes, we marvel at this priceless gift that has been wonderfully made and entrusted to us and to the world (Ps. 139:13–14). While we are enraptured in the wonder of it all, a precious little child whom we immediately love beyond words will also mean for us sleep deprivation, lots of work, and constant attention. Yet when I observe parents and grandparents of small children, I seldom hear complaints but rather observe the joy they experience and the love they embody in innumerable and sacrificial ways each and every day.

It means a whole lot of work for God to create the world he loves. In creation, God unleashes his love in space and time. In love, God speaks the world into existence. From his first loving creative act, the very language for God communicates that he is a relational worker. Father, Son, and Holy Spirit are present in the work of creation. As the Spirit of God hovers over the waters, a collaborative and creative God speaks light and life into existence. We explicitly read in the New Testament that Jesus Christ, the second member of the Trinity, is actively involved in original creation. Jesus is the one who will come to redeem the now broken world he had once made perfectly.

It is no wonder that as the triune God lovingly creates the heavens and earth, he says, "Oh, that's good." This refrain continues throughout the Genesis creation account. This loving God really enjoys his work; he delights in forming and crafting the material stuff of this world. Between the lines of Genesis 1, there seems to be a celebratory playfulness to God's work, a divine enjoyment that comes in the satisfaction not only of a job well done but of great trinitarian collaboration and mutual honor.

Often when I meet people, I not only ask them their names but also ask them to tell me their life stories and the work they do. As they describe their work, it is not unusual to see a glimmer in their

11

eyes and a smile on their face. When I ask them to tell me what they like about their work, many describe a joyful satisfaction in what they have been called to do for such a large portion of their lives. My hunch is that even though there are parts of any job that are unenjoyable, most of us get satisfaction and a sense of accomplishment in our callings and career paths. Why? When we experience joy in our work, we resonate with our creation design; we hear in our hearts the distant echoes of Eden.

After creating an orderly environment, God speaks life into existence, and it is to have a life of its own. "Then God said, 'Let the earth produce vegetation: seed-bearing plants and fruit trees on the earth bearing fruit with seed in it according to their kinds.' And it was so" (Gen. 1:11). God creates plants to be germinative, to be productive beyond themselves, not dissimilar to how he reaches beyond himself. God is fruitful, as is the life he creates. How that life develops, and what that life becomes, determines the kind of fruit that it brings forth. Yet even with all this brilliance and beauty, God's creation, consisting of plant and animal life in an environment for their flourishing, is still quite incomplete.

It is here in the Genesis account of creation that humankind, the crown of creation, emerges in the garden. God's unique role for humanity in creation is to be his governors—that is, his rulers, overseers, managers, or stewards in charge of the works of his hands (Ps. 8:6). At the end of each day on which God works, he stops to look at what he has made and sees that it is "good." But on the day God creates humankind, he looks at his crown of creation and sees that it is "very good" (Gen. 1:31). It is as if God is acknowledging that this is the masterpiece of his creation, made in his very image. In creation's breathtakingly beautiful symphony, we are the grand finale.

A Big Job Description

When we are searching or interviewing for a job, understanding the job description is essential. A job description frames the

responsibilities, duties, values, expectations, and reporting relationships that the work entails. A job description offers both clarity
about and accountability for our work. In God's story of work, his
image bearers are given a job description. In Genesis 1 we read,
"Then God said, 'Let Us make man in Our image, according to
Our likeness; and let them rule over the fish of the sea and over the
birds of the sky and over the livestock and over all the earth, and
over every crawling thing that crawls on the earth.' God created
man in His own image, in the image of God He created him; male
and female He created them. God blessed them; and God said to
them, 'Be fruitful and multiply, and fill the earth, and subdue it;
and rule over the fish of the sea and over the birds of the sky and
over every living thing that moves on the earth'" (Gen. 1:26–28
NASB). At the very heart of God's job description for humanity is
our commission to exercise dominion over creation. Within God's
design we as humans, his image bearers, are given unique capabil-
ity, capacity, and authority to carry out this important role. In any
good organizational design and job description, our authority and
responsibility must be commensurate. We are not made responsible
for something without the proper authority to fulfill it. Within his
creation design, God gives humans both great responsibility and
great authority. In doing so, God places a unique and distinguish-
ing stamp that sets us apart from the rest of creation: his likeness
and image.

Made in his very image, we are made to connect with God, to
experience intimacy with him, and to reflect his creativity in our
work. We are created to know God, be known by him, and work
as he works. As beings created in the image of God, our purpose is
to bring our lives into conformity with his purposes and as a result
uniquely reflect who God is to his good world. In your Monday
world of both paid and unpaid work, you are called and empowered
to display a glimpse of God's glory in your work and to those around
you. As an image bearer, you are created to relate with God and to
reflect God in all that you are and do.

We often marvel when children look like and have the manner-isms of their family members. As we get older and look in the mir-ror or through a family photo album, we begin to see our parents looking back at us. With the passage of time, our genetic blueprint given to us by our parents emerges with unmistakable and often uncanny detail. In that sense we are a spitting image of our parents, reflecting who has brought us into the world and shaped us in so many ways. In a similar way, as the crown of creation made in the image of God, we reflect our Creator to the world. This does not mean that we are little gods or deities. There will always be a clear distinction between the divine Creator and our creaturely nature. Yet God's imaging stamp on us gives us unfathomable intrinsic value, great importance, and unique stewardship within creation.

Our importance as his image bearers cannot be overstated. We are entrusted to rule with God, aligning our work with his divine will and kingdom. For example, when we say in the Lord's Prayer that God's will may be done on earth as it is in heaven, we are re-flecting his creation design, aligning our will and work with God's. Our image-bearing reveals that God is a ruler and a worker who reveals himself in creative goodness. God's motivation for work is love, so this must also be our motivation: to love him, our neighbors, and our world in and through the work we are called and com-missioned to do in our Monday worlds. We are to rule, to exercise dominion, out of love, not out of ruthless domination. The first humans were entrusted with fish, birds, cattle, and creeping things; most of us today do not spend time caring for animals, but we all are entrusted with this same charge to rule. Our rule today may instead be over property, computers, phones, art, emails, spreadsheets, dia-pers, meals, transportation, manufacturing, financial portfolios, car maintenance, tools, wood, nails, or lawn mowers.

The job description given to humankind involves not only ruling and exercising loving dominion but also being fruitful. The Bible describes this twofold aspect of fruitfulness as the fruit of the womb and the fruit of the land. In Deuteronomy we read, "The LORD will

14

make you prosper abundantly with offspring, the offspring of your livestock, and your land's produce in the land the LORD swore to your ancestors to give you" (Deut. 28:11). Humans are to be fruitful both in having children and in doing good work for the glory of God and the good of others.

The Fruitfulness of Work

As God's story unfolds in Genesis 2, we're given more texture as to how his image bearers are to be fruitful. This command to be fruitful is facilitated by our relational connection to God. Fruitfulness flows from relationship. The garden God first placed human beings in was idyllic and particularly well suited for their flourishing, but their true environment of flourishing was and is God himself.

Humans are created to be with God like our lungs are created to be filled with air. Without air, without God, we cannot survive for long.[4] This is the natural order God established: fruitfulness is tied to relationships, to loving cooperation and collaboration, to a right and good environment. Consider a peach tree. By God's design, it succeeds in bringing forth fruit when the conditions are right, but it flourishes most in a grove of peach trees. The right nourishing environment, the right ecosystem, the right nutrients, and the right soil are all important. In a similar way, our work requires a right, good, and collaborative environment to bring forth fruitfulness.

Likewise, humans are created to partner with God, to rule and govern with him, to accomplish his agenda of love, and to cooperate with other human beings with love as our goal. Ruling in God's image, we are successful when we, too, pursue creative goodness for both the creation and the people who inhabit it. The conditions required for human fruitfulness in their vocation is described as the kingdom of God, which simply means the reign of God, the effective range of his sovereign will. Put simply, ruling over creation succeeds when we rule in love with the ultimate ruler, and ruling over creation fails when we don't. As human beings we are commissioned to rule with the ultimate ruler, align our will and work within his kingdom purposes, and bear fruit for him.

Genesis 2 emphasizes God's design for humanity and the significant contribution that we, the crown of creation, are to make in his world. Prior to God forming man from the dust of the earth and breathing life into him, a surprising tension emerges regarding the incompleteness of God's creation. We read that "there was no man to work the ground" (Gen. 2:5). This means that the earth itself was created in order for humans to cultivate and shape it. God desires that there be harmonious human cooperation within creation. Not only do we, the crown of creation, have joyful intimacy with our Creator but we also are asked to joyfully contribute to the ongoing creative, beautiful, and sustaining work of God in his world.

What Is Work?

When we hear the word "work," we often think of what we are paid to do. Of course, getting paid is important to make a living, but work is not limited to what we are paid to do. Work is not defined by its compensation but by its contribution to others. Work is not first and foremost about economic exchange, financial remuneration, or a pathway to wish fulfillment; rather, it is about God-honoring creativity and loving contribution. When we work, we contribute value. Like our Maker, we contribute value by "making." Our work, whatever God has called us to do, whatever it is, wherever it is done, whether or not we are paid for it, is our God-honoring, loving, beauty-making contribution to others and to the world. Work is integral to being human, essential to loving God and his created world, and vital to loving neighbors.[5]

In Genesis 2 we read, "The LORD God took the man and put him in the garden of Eden to work it and keep it" (2:15 ESV). Work is meant to cultivate and nurture creation as well as to protect it. In work we create, form, arrange, and rearrange, but we also preserve and protect. God's work in creating human beings in particular tells us something important: God invites partnership, co-creation, and collaboration. Unlike many of us who wear ourselves out, unwilling to hand over our work to others, God delegates and empowers the crown of his creation. God welcomes human beings into his garden and says, in effect, "Now you try. Tend and protect the garden I have planted. Join with me in this beautiful work I have started."

Reflecting on God's story of work, Rabbi Abraham Heschel speaks insightfully about the inherent goodness of work and what that means for our intrinsic value as humans: "Labor is not only the destiny of man; it is endowed with divine dignity."[6] Embodying creative goodness, we are to be fruitful in our contribution.

We are called not only to the essential work of tending and making things but also to culture creation. Andy Crouch invites us to take a stewardship posture anchored in what he refers to as culture making. The stewardship of culture making involves both cultivators and creators. Crouch describes cultivators as "people who tend and nourish what is best in human culture, who do the hard and painstaking work to preserve the best of what people before us have done." Creators, he says, are "people who dare to think and do something that has never been thought or done before, something that makes the world more welcoming and thrilling and beautiful."[7] Humanity's creative work is varied, broad, and far-reaching. We not only make or fix things but actively create and cultivate culture. Cultural artifacts include visual art, music, menus, technologies, budgets, strategic plans, games, and sports, all of which reflect the immense creativity and beauty-making potential we image bearers possess. In innumerable ways, we are created to create and make beauty in the world, and we do this not in isolation but in community.

What really makes our creative work sing is our collaboration with each other. By working together, we can have a far greater impact than if we operated alone. In Genesis 2, a beautiful picture of collaboration between God and human emerges: "And out of the ground the LORD God formed every animal of the field and every bird of the sky, and brought them to the man to see what he would call them; and whatever the man called a living creature, that was its name. The man gave names to all the livestock, and to the birds of the sky, and to every animal of the field" (Gen. 2:19–20 NASB). What is God doing when he entrusts the naming of animals to Adam? Why doesn't God just tell him what the names are? Instead, he tells Adam to come up with them. Adam's work of naming is essential to exercising dominion, actively ruling and unleashing creativity. Just as God speaks and things happen, so we human beings speak to make things happen. While God speaks material reality from nothing, we as his image bearers take the ingredients of original creation, fashioning them in innumerable ways and forms.

In addition to the work of cultivating and tending of the garden with their hands, God also entrusts imaginative work to us, designing various technologies and things of beauty and goodness. In God's creation design, we see an equal affirmation of all kinds of work, whether manual or conceptual, whether done on a busy city street or in an office building. We humans are to dig, to cultivate, to garden, to get our hands dirty as we creatively make things out of the earth that God has already made. But we also are called to name the animals and thus create categories and work with ideas. All these forms of thought, imagination, speech, and activity are means of exercising rule. Adam's naming of the animals shows that both our ruling and our fruitfulness stem from our collaboration with God. And this co-creating with God is meant to extend to other people. Human collaboration with God begets collaboration with other people.

Created for Community

It is important to note that, just as God acknowledged the incompleteness of his creation without humans to work the ground, he notes one person's incompleteness without another: "It is not good for the man to be alone. I will make a helper corresponding to him" (Gen. 2:18). Adam needs a helper. The Bible's use of "helper" does not connote inferiority but rather an equal partner. But is this a helper for *who* or a helper for *what*? In a real sense the answer is both. The first woman, Eve, comes forth as Adam's help and companion not only so he can experience relational intimacy but also so he can be a more effective and fruitful worker. Eve's design is tied to more than her compatibility with Adam; she is to be a collaborator in the human job description.[8]

Humankind's job description is too big for Adam to do alone. The animals might prove to be helpful for Adam's work but are ultimately woefully insufficient for that big job description. Thus, the first marriage relationship is also the first co-creative, collaborative work relationship. In the garden of Eden, Adam and Eve operate out of the plenteousness of collaboration with God. There is plenty of goodness to go around. There is no shortage. There is no pretense. There is utter transparency. They have nothing to hide. There is no need to exert one's will over another's, nor to withdraw from each other. They are to recognize their connection to each other and rejoice in that partnership. This is a picture not only of an ideal marriage but also of an ideal working relationship. An essential aspect of their work is to help each other do great work and to flourish in their calling to exercise dominion and be fruitful.

In exploring the beginnings of God's work story, it becomes evident that we are created with community in mind, to work with others who bring needed wisdom, gifts, and abilities to our work. While we may or may not do daily work directly with others, work was never designed as a solitary enterprise. None of us can be truly productive unless we work with others. And a good portion of our satisfaction at work comes from the relational connections that emerge and deepen in our workplaces.

I am confident that, when you think of your work, the relationships you develop over time are one of the things you enjoy most. As I interact with people from all walks of life, a consistent refrain I hear is that they love the people they get to know and work with as they nourish creativity, solve problems, and accomplish organizational goals. Retirees often tell me what they miss most is not the work they did but the colleagues they left behind. Much of God's good design for your work is not only the work itself but the other image bearers who are working with you in your Monday world.

Work as Worship

Work undertaken as God designed it is a form of worship. We often think of worship as what we do on Sunday and work as what we do on Monday. But in God's original design we do not find a gap between Sunday and Monday. Creation design reflects a seamlessness of work, worship, and rest. While we are not to worship our work—that is idolatry—work is a vital aspect of God-honoring worship.

The language of work as cultivation and creation in Genesis 2 is embedded in the Hebrew word *avodah*, which is translated as "to cultivate" (2:15 NASB). The Old Testament elsewhere renders *avodah* in various ways—as "work," "service," or "craftsmanship" in many instances, yet other times as "worship." The various usages of this Hebrew word tell us that God's original design and desire is that our work and our worship be seamlessly integrated.[9] Properly understood, our work is to be thoughtfully woven into the integral fabric of our worship, for God designs and intends our work, our vocational calling, to be an act of God-honoring worship.

In the book of Exodus, God frames the work of the people of Israel as having a priestly function: "Now then, if you will indeed obey My voice and keep My covenant, then you shall be My own possession among all the peoples, for all the earth is Mine; you shall be to Me a kingdom of priests and a holy nation" (19:5–6 NASB). While some in Israel serve as priests in the tabernacle, here we see that all image bearers have a priestly identity in God's kingdom. God, in effect, says to all Israel as priests, You are going to show the world what my character is like and point others to me.

Most of us don't think of ourselves as pastors, clergy, or priests, but if we grasp God's original creation design and Jesus's kingdom reign in the world, we will live joyfully and expectantly into that identity. In many ways the garden of Eden was designed as a temple of worship, and we as image bearers are created to have a priestly role exhibiting complete trust in God, a faithful presence, communing prayer, and joyful praise. Our God-honoring work is designed to show off the beautiful existence and glory of our Creator.

Work and Rest

The Genesis writer tells us that, having concluded with his great masterpiece of humanity, the apex of creation, God rests from all of his work. It isn't that God is tired or done with all his creative endeavors. In Sabbath rest, God stops working to delight in his trinitarian relationship and in all that had been made. God works for six days and then rests for one day.

As his image bearers, we are to embrace this divine rhythm of work and rest. When we work within creation design, emulating God's example, we also are disciplined and diligent to take our rest. When we work in God's way, we joyfully experience regular rest. None of creation can flourish without rest. The work-and-rest rhythm built into creation design is so important that God reemphasizes Sabbath when giving his covenant people the Ten Commandments. God anchors the law of the Sabbath within creation design: "Remember the Sabbath day, to keep it holy: You are to labor six days and do all your work, but the seventh day is a Sabbath to the LORD your God. You must not do any work—you, your son or daughter, your male or female servant, your livestock, or the resident alien who is within your city gates. For the LORD made the heavens and the earth, the sea, and everything in them in six days; then he rested on the seventh day. Therefore the LORD blessed the Sabbath day and declared it holy" (Exod. 20:8–11). Heschel writes, "The Sabbath as a day of abstaining from work is not a depreciation but an affirmation of labor, a divine exaltation of its dignity."[10] Sabbath is a space for delight and celebration, restoring the soul and fostering intimacy with God and others. The Sabbath is also a way for human beings to abandon work outcomes to God and to trust that his care and provision will continue even if we don't take everything into our own hands. As such, Sabbath is an act of trust. Adam and Eve experienced both beautiful work and beautiful rest in the garden of Eden.

The first two chapters of Genesis give us an extraordinary story of God's original design for work. Truly, this is a picture of what our work ought to be, a stunning blueprint of how God designs our Monday world. Yet presently our work and workplaces aren't what they were designed to be. Work has badly gone awry. In God's good story of work, we now encounter great tragedy. It is to this tragedy we now turn.

A Prayer for Our Work

Let your work be seen by your servants, and your splendor by their children. Let the favor of the Lord our God be on us; establish for us the work of our hands—establish the work of our hands! (Psalm 90:16–17)

Questions for Reflection and Discussion

Take a few minutes to read through Genesis 1 and 2.

- Why does grasping the big *why* of work matter so much?
- How does knowing God is the first worker change the way you view work?
- How does knowing a God who works (and works with us) deepen your intimacy with him in your workplace?
- In what ways does your work image God's creative work?
- In what ways does your work serve to create and cultivate culture?

2

Work's Great Tragedy

God's curse after the Fall expresses the fact that alienation is inherent to the human experience of work.

—Miroslav Volf[1]

One of the reasons I love country music is that it captures the raw brokenness we experience in our daily work. Our work is a far cry from Eden. Creation's once beautiful and perfectly tuned symphony has become a discordant dirge. Songs like Merle Haggard's "Workin' Man Blues," Johnny Paycheck's "Take This Job and Shove It," and Alan Jackson and Jimmy Buffett's "It's 5 O'Clock Somewhere" capture the emotional and visceral angst we often feel in our workplaces.

Many of us can relate with this kind of frustration in our workplaces, where each day may be a reminder of how we are undervalued, how we are underemployed or underpaid, how our supervisor is not trusting, how our job itself has been poorly structured, how we're not getting recognition, or how no one sees or seems to care enough to support us or our ideas. It doesn't matter if our workplace is at home with children, teaching in a classroom, or laboring on a factory floor, under the hood of a car, in a crawl space fixing a pipe, or on a computer in an office—work can be a source of great frustration in our lives. Dealing with difficult customers, treating a persistent disease, or serving a demanding boss is a big pain. Having to let an employee go or downsize a labor force can be agonizing. Facing a family's mountain of dirty laundry can feel insurmountable. Work can bring discouragement and seem difficult if not impossible.

Those country artists have an important point. Our work is not what it ought to be. We feel it deep within us. Country musician Jelly Roll put it well: we and our world are damaged beyond repair.[2] What on earth happened to work? Theologians describe the great tragedy that affected our work and everything else as the fall. God's design for humans, for creation, and for work became corrupted, disfigured, and disintegrated. As a consequence of sin, death and destruction entered the world. Tragedy visited paradise.

Paradise Lost

The story of tragedy visiting paradise is described in Genesis 3. Before we explore it, let's recall the beautiful picture painted for us in Genesis 1 and 2. Adam and Eve are lovingly, harmoniously, creatively, and collaboratively working in the garden of Eden. As they work, Adam and Eve trust God and experience intimacy with him and with each other. They worship God in and through their work. Their work in the garden brings satisfaction and delight. As they embrace creation's design of work and rest, there is no sense of frustration, exhaustion, conflict, toil, or pain. But this all changes when we come to chapter 3.

The serpent appears, peddling a glittering counterfeit to fruitful work with God. To make it enticing, the serpent begins by attempting to impeach God's trustworthiness, saying, "Did God really say, 'You can't eat from any tree in the garden'?" (Gen. 3:1). The deceptive message is this: you can't trust God, and you can't trust what he said. Lured by Satan's lies, Adam and Eve commit an unthinkable and unconscionable act of disobedient folly. In eating the fruit of the tree of the knowledge of good and evil, Adam and Eve rebel against God and join a cosmic conspiracy. Sin, shame, and death enter God's good world, disintegrating and corrupting his perfect creation design. Paradise is lost, and sin wreaks a devastating effect on humans and their work. God's big job description for human beings to rule and to work with him left open the contingency that they might decide to rule and to work with or without him. Adam and Eve are deceived into deciding to work without God. In a grand mystery that is hard for us to grasp, God allows evil to have a place in our world, and the Evil One exploits this contingency with devastating consequences. God expels Adam and Eve from the garden of Eden, yet they are to continue to work, but now in vastly different conditions: "So the LORD God sent him away from the garden of Eden to work the ground from which he was taken" (Gen. 3:23).[3] While deep within us there are still distant longings for Eden, like Adam and Eve, we now work in a post-Eden world.

The Genesis writer clearly tells us that while work is not a *result* of the tragedy that wreaked unimaginable havoc in paradise, work is profoundly impacted by it. After Adam and Eve's act of disobedience, shame permeates their lives and their work. God comes to them in the garden, and they attempt to hide from him. Recognizing their shame and responding to their disobedience and rebellion, God speaks to Adam and Eve about their work, how it has fundamentally changed, and the destiny of death that now awaits them. "And he said to the man, 'Because you listened to your wife and ate from the tree about which I commanded you, "Do not eat from it": The ground is cursed because of you. You will eat from it by means of painful labor all the days of your life. It will produce thorns and thistles for you, and you will eat the plants of the field. You will eat bread by the sweat of your brow until you return to the ground, since you were taken from it. For you are dust, and you will return to dust'" (Gen. 3:17–19). The Genesis writer employs the word "curse" to describe the new chilling reality and its devastating

25

effects on work. In our context, the word "curse" often brings to mind images of a kind of mystical hocus-pocus, like someone casting spells in a Harry Potter movie or the Wicked Witch of the West in *The Wizard of Oz*. Though I don't want to minimize the very real presence and power of Satan, evil, demons, and occult practices, the word "curse" here does not mean a kind of occultist spell. Rather, a careful look at Genesis reveals far-reaching and long-lasting changes regarding our work and the conditions in which it takes place. Sin's scourge on work means the very nature of human work has been greatly altered, and the human job description to be fruitful is now deeply frustrated and greatly hindered. Under the curse, work has a new persistent and agonizing dimension to it. It is now toilsome and difficult. Thorns and thistles bring the sweat of exertion to the human brow.

I really enjoy gardening and working in the yard. I love the aroma of freshly cut grass and the delightful fragrances of beautiful backyard flowers permeating the crisp morning air. While gardening brings enjoyment and satisfaction, it also has its share of frustrating weeds to pull and persistent pests to confront. There are hot summer days when my garden work is not so great. With sweat beading on my forehead and my muscles aching, it feels a lot like what the Genesis writer describes in chapter 3. Yet much more is going on besides work's thorny challenges.

As we read further in Genesis 3, we feel the intensity of hurricane-force winds rearranging the entire landscape of human existence, including the fruitfulness tied to both human productivity and pro-creativity. When we read further in Genesis 4, instead of loving co-operation and collaboration, we encounter competition, resentment, shame, and envy. Workplace relationships now exhibit lovelessness, often taking the form of either emotional and verbal attack or relational withdrawal.[4] This attack and withdrawal ultimately culminates in cold-blooded hatred that often leads to violence, abuse, or power over others. We shudder and grieve when we hear of a disgruntled employee walking into a workplace and gunning down colleagues. This violence is not new in human history. The first murder recorded in the Bible occurs in the workplace: Cain murders his brother Abel out in the field (Gen. 4:1–8). By the time we reach Genesis 4, human work only continues to spiral downward into the dark black hole of arrogance and ambition. Here we encounter the tower of Babel.

The Babel Debacle

Having been expelled from the garden, fallen image bearers choose to pursue life and work without God and for their own purposes and glory instead of his. The Genesis writer captures this ambitious work project and its self-centered motivation: "And they said, 'Come, let's build ourselves a city and a tower with its top in the sky. Let's make a name for ourselves; otherwise, we will be scattered throughout the earth'" (Gen. 11:4). Employing the hard work of their hands, their image-bearing creativity, and the emerging tools of their technology, fallen humans build the tower of Babel, working as if God were completely absent.

Somehow, they deceive themselves into believing that the mighty work of their hands, this grand tower, will give them an identity, deeper meaning, and transcendent significance. Rather than collaborating with God, they work without him, collaborating with nothing but their human abilities. Dallas Willard gets to the heart of the matter of the Babel debacle and its rebellious paradigm of human work gone awry: "Babel represents human efforts to succeed by human abilities."[5] While Babel occurred at a point in history and God intervened to thwart it, the tower also universally represents self-sufficient humans rejecting God in their lives and in their work. A Babel mindset is often present in our daily work; we treat God as though he is completely out of the equation, a non-factor. We often work as if God does not exist, as if work is all about us.

This kind of Babel mindset today might be embodied by a CEO, a manager, or an organizational leader whose dominating motivation and highest goal is to make a name for themself. They are bent on advancing their career and gaining greater power at the cost of all other workplace stakeholders. They focus on short-term gains, quickly raising profits not to benefit the company but instead for their next promotion. Maximum revenue and shareholder value are the only real goals, and broader considerations of human flourishing are more or less nonessential. It doesn't take long to see these leaders are more than willing to leave behind innumerable casualties. In such situations, those in power fulfill their own desires, resulting in injustice and exploitation. They abuse their workers and poorly steward the earth's resources to maximize profit. Much of this profit ends up in their pockets, while those at the lower rungs of the organization can barely eke out a living wage. And across the world, those with less power and control languish and do not get to realize their flourishing potential as image bearers of God. With a Babel mindset, corrupt power dynamics in our work and workplaces become all too common.

Work's Downward Spiral

As God's story of work continues throughout the Bible, we read of sin's downward spiral beyond corrupted power dynamics. We hear the heartfelt struggle of work, its gnawing sense of sheer futility (Eccles. 2:17–20). We regularly encounter the exhausting *weariness* of work. Work has become a heavy yoke we were not meant to bear. The vivid biblical imagery of the curse paints the dire picture of the far-reaching and devastating consequences of human rebellion against a good, just, and holy God.

C. S. Lewis brilliantly captures the curse of work in *The Lion, the Witch and the Wardrobe*. Lewis's mythical Narnia once displayed the vibrant and flourishing warmth of summer, but now it faces the chill of winter. One of Lewis's main characters, a young girl named Lucy, questions Mr. Tumnus about the White Witch whose curse has so dreadfully altered the land. This curse meant that it was always winter and never Christmas. Lucy gives an incredulous response to such a dreadful thing. Lewis reminds us we live and work in a fallen world where it is always winter and never Christmas. In this cursed world, we are alienated from God, from other human beings, and from the good work we were created to do. We are broken people who live and work with other broken people and within broken systems. In some cases, workplaces and entire industries become fundamentally corrupt and oppose God's ways and human flourishing. Work in every dimension has gone badly awry. Our work is not what it ought to be. In the painful aspects of our work, we join with fallen creation in its groanings.

When it comes to pain, I would rather not be there when it happens. I will never forget the time when, in a hurry to get to an appointment, I slammed my car door shut before my right hand had made it out of the car. My crushed fingers radiated pain through my body that was so intense I almost blacked out. After retrieving my crushed and quite bruised fingers from the door and wrapping my hand in ice, my swollen fingers throbbed for hours. When we experience excruciating pain from a physical injury or the despairing emotional pain of a devastating loss, our visceral and instinctual reaction is often a groan.

This, too, is true of all of creation in a post-Eden world. In his letter to a group of first-century followers of Jesus in Rome, the apostle Paul makes the point that we, along with cursed and fallen creation, feel the pain of alienation from our Creator. We hear Eden's heartbreaking song. On the one hand, with a sense of hope flowing through his inspired speech, Paul looks to the transforming power of the gospel and the glorious future of redemption. But on the other he describes an inherent groaning, one that presently permeates every aspect of our lives, our work, and our world. Paul writes, "For we know that the whole creation has been groaning together with labor pains until now. Not only that, but we ourselves who have the Spirit as the firstfruits—we also groan within ourselves, eagerly waiting for adoption, the redemption of our bodies" (Rom. 8:22–23).

Paul strikes many rich theological notes in these verses, but for our purposes, his metaphor of childbirth is particularly instructive. Childbirth is a joyful thing, but it is also a painful thing. I will never forget when my two children were born. Observing my wife endure the painful struggle of labor, she quickly catapulted to a heroic status. Yes, there was great joy when our children were born. But there was also a whole lot of pain and struggle until we got to that point. In this moment of redemptive history, our work and workplaces are filled with difficulty and pain. Someday this will not be the case, but for now we must not expect otherwise. Our work provokes some painful groaning.

Painfully Difficult Work

When sin entered the world and corrupted God's design, it made the very nature of work itself harder, even painfully difficult. The workplace systems, technologies, economics, pressures, and organizational structures we deal with every day reflect a broken world. We encounter difficult people in the workplace. We also regularly encounter backstabbing and political maneuvering. We observe co-workers playing power games with the boss to their own advantage. We face intense dog-eat-dog competition on a global scale. Government regulation and the constant threat of possible litigation bring new complexities and greater demands to our work. An increasing level of uncertainty and unpredictability is more the norm of our workplaces in a fast-changing world, and with it comes greater anxiety and fear. Adapting to new, game-changing technologies requires continual learning and resource investment. Finding quality and skilled workers in a competitive labor market is exasperating. Remote working has its own strengths and weaknesses and has greatly changed the contours of the marketplace.

Some workplaces can be toxic and even abusive. If abuse occurs, human resource and legal professionals should get involved. If you are in a workplace in which you come away the majority of the time feeling bad, go to the people who know you best to examine the situation with you. Don't go through it alone. We need each other for confidential and transparent reality checks and exploration of options.

I received an email from a friend who described his work in the highly competitive global corporate world. Facing the pressures of staff reductions and ever-increasing sales targets in a global economic downturn, he describes a battlefield environment: "The goals are extraordinarily difficult to complete. Morale suffers under the carnage." The environment many of us work in every day can only be described as a small-scale war zone. We can face years with long hours of backbreaking work, sometimes without adequate protection for injury or while inhaling toxic fumes. In some jobs, we can feel like a cog in a machine, doing exhausting, repetitive, often underappreciated tasks with low compensation. There is a lot of groaning in our work.

Work is painfully difficult when we have to do jobs that are less than desirable. One of my first employment experiences was putting in long hours at a fast-food restaurant. Being given the task of cleaning the bathrooms was not my idea of fun, but someone had to do it. I think that's why I like the show *Dirty Jobs*. Mike Rowe, the host, takes on the jobs no one wants, from rattlesnake catching to septic tank cleaning. Imagine the job of being a roadkill collector. Here is Rowe's job listing: "Must be able to work long hours braving oncoming traffic while picking up creatures of various size and breed and in various states of decay. Benefits include working outdoors. Strong stomach a plus!" I am not sure Rowe has had a lot of takers on this one, but in a fallen world, someone has to collect roadkill. The curse of the fall means our work is often painfully difficult.

The work we do can also feel empty and meaningless. In a globally interconnected economy, a good deal of our labor is far removed from the beneficiaries of our work. Because of this distance, we do not receive the inherent satisfaction of seeing the direct benefit of our work. When I speak with people about their work, I often hear people plead, "Tom, please tell me that what I do every day really matters." Behind these words lurks a haunting sense that our work really does not have much significance. The Old Testament book of Ecclesiastes addresses the disillusionment that is part of our daily experience in this fallen world. The author's pursuit of power, pleasure, and material comforts leads him to the conclusion that it is all for naught. Satisfaction and fulfillment elude him in his pursuits, particularly his work.

The writer of Ecclesiastes describes his disillusionment with work in a fallen world as futile and striving after wind: "Therefore, I hated life because the work that was done under the sun was distressing to me. For everything is futile and a pursuit of the wind. I hated all my work that I labored at under the sun because I must leave it to the one who comes after me. . . . For what does a person get with all his work and all his efforts that he labors at under the sun? For all his days are filled with grief, and his occupation is sorrowful; even at night, his mind does not rest. This too is futile" (Eccles. 2:17–18, 22–23). Even though we may enjoy a good deal of our work, there are moments we, too, feel much the same way. We wonder whether our work really matters for more than a fleeting glimpse of human history.

The Idolatry of Workaholism

Difficulty and disillusionment can distort how we see our work. Rather than worship God through our work, we can easily and subtly begin to slip into idolatry and to worship our work. An idol is anything or anyone that we make ultimate in our lives rather than God. The most destructive and dangerous idols we worship are the idols that lurk in our hearts. But Scripture is clear: God will not share his glory with anyone or anything. God does not stutter when he declares, "Do not have other gods besides me" (Exod. 20:3). God will not allow any rivals. Our ultimate allegiance, the greatest love of our hearts, is God and God only. Yet our work itself can become that which is most important in our lives and bring with it spiritual poverty and enslavement.

One of the more common ways we make work an idol is through workaholism. Workaholism—literally an addiction to work despite costs to our health, relationships, and peace of mind—often points to a deeper idolatry in our lives. In this common form of idolatry, our entire life and identity center on what we do. Work idolatry can be driven by our pursuit of the American Dream, of material comforts, of financial security, or of our attempts to prop up a certain image of success. Our work idolatry can surface as a convenient distraction from matters of our soul that need attention or from messy relationships and conflict we want to avoid. Work idolatry is often concealed in the language of organizational loyalty and commitment and is regularly legitimized in a competitive work environment as the required pathway to promotion and advancement. Workaholism can also be driven by overextended living, materialism, and rebellion against God. Regardless of the form it takes, like a black hole from which light cannot escape, excessive devotion to work smothers the soul. Workaholism inevitably extracts a heavy toll from our well-being and crowds out our relationships with God and others.

In the New Testament, Jesus tells the story of someone whose life was consumed with work. In material terms, his work brought him great success. In his first-century agrarian economy, he had gained so many goods that he had to build bigger buildings just to store everything. All his work and his stuff crowded out his relationships with God and his neighbors. Jesus strongly indicts this man whose work consumed him, who lived and worked as if God did not exist, who thought he had it all, but who at the end of the day had nothing of eternal worth. In a sudden and unexpected death this man left his work and all he had accumulated behind. In Jesus's telling of the story, God describes him as the ultimate fool: "You fool! This very night your life is demanded of you. And the things you have prepared—whose will they be?" (Luke 12:20). Jesus gives us the strongest of warnings about the blinding peril of a life lived without God, one that embraces an idolatrous view of work and worships self and personal comfort.

Workaholism is a foolish way to live. Sometimes this way of life is fueled by our own insecurities and is reinforced in our culture as a strong work ethic. This distortion of work wreaks havoc on our physical, emotional, and spiritual health as well as our relationships. The sin of a hurried, harried, and preoccupied work life is often the default mode in our fast-paced, competitive world. Much of this frantic pace is driven by our distorted view of work. When our work is out of whack, our life will be out of whack too.

Other times, however, instead of making too much of our work, we make too little of it. When work is distorted in this way, we easily make leisure an idol. Inclined toward slothfulness, we may find creative excuses not to do our work or perhaps we will do just enough to get by to keep our job and get a regular paycheck. A slothful life is a serious problem in which we neglect our God-given work. Slothfulness violates our very image-bearing nature and leads us to rely on the hard work and industry of others and to develop a sense of entitlement. At its core, slothfulness is a self-centered resistance to what love requires. It is all too easy for a college student whose parents are footing the tuition bill to party away their college years, taking for granted their parents' hard work that has made a college education possible. But it is not only younger adults who can live a slothful life; older retired adults can do this as well. The common notion of a long, leisurely, and self-indulgent retirement in many ways reflects the distortion of slothfulness.

The Bible repeatedly warns of this peril. The writer of Proverbs declares, "The slacker does not plow during planting season; at harvest time he looks, and there is nothing" (Prov. 20:4). Slothfulness is a glaring corruption of God's design for our lives and his good world.

Challenging Work Dualism

We were made for an integrated life of work and worship. One of the great tragedies of humanity's fall is the distortion of dualism, which, put simply, is wrongly dividing something that should not be divided. Dualism is a common distortion of our understanding of work. When we wrongly distinguish one type of work from another, placing value on some types of work at the expense of others, we fall into the distortion of work dualism. Work dualism sees through a bifurcated lens in the form of a two-story world. The upper story is seen as a higher vocational calling, one devoted to the church or "religious" or "sacred" work. The lower story is viewed as a lower vocational calling, one devoted to "secular" work. This dualistic distortion is often perpetuated with subtle and spiritual-sounding words. In the fourth century, the theologian and bishop Augustine of Hippo spoke of the contemplative life versus the active life. The contemplative life was given to sacred things and deemed a higher calling, while the active life was given to secular things and regarded as a lower calling. This kind of thinking helped spawn a distorted view of work that continues in Christian communities today.

Work dualism can be seen in various Christian traditions. For example, the language of "full-time Christian work" is commonly used to describe those who are called to be a pastor, missionary, or nonprofit worker. However, a proper biblical understanding of work is that all Christians are called to "full-time Christian work," doing their work well for the glory of God, regardless of their specific vocation.

It wasn't long after I began my pastoral work that a lady approached me after a Sunday worship service to share how meaningful the sermon was. I was grateful for her warm and affirming words, but then she asked me, "Pastor, when did you receive your call?" I replied in a polite manner, but her carefully nuanced words reflected this common distortion about work. I wanted to ask her, "Tell me, when did you receive your call?" She seemed to believe that my calling to pastoral work was more important than the work she had been doing for years.

Many followers of Jesus go their entire careers with the suffocating distortion that their work is not as important and God-honoring as that of a pastor or missionary. Work dualism often prompts well-meaning people to leave the work to which they are uniquely called to pursue a "higher calling." The monastic impulse of followers of Jesus to withdraw from the normal day-to-day world to pursue a contemplative life in "sacred spaces" reflects this distortion. In reality, there is no more sacred space than the workplace where God has called you to serve him as you love your neighbor and serve the common good.

Perpetuating this work dualism reinforces the false two-story work world, in which certain vocations are elevated over others, and bolsters the unbiblical idea of withdrawing from the world rather than engaging it and being faithfully present in it. Work dualism raises its distorted head when some work we may be called to do is perceived as beneath us or not a good use of our gifts. As I interact with people in the middle years of life, I hear a subtle work dualism emerge from the shadows of well-meaning hearts as they pursue work they believe will somehow be more pleasing to God or more eternally important than what they were doing in earlier stages of their career. Many think that a move to the nonprofit sector will be a transition from a "life of success" to a "life of significance," when the reality is that significance is available to followers of Jesus in whatever work God has placed them. Because of sin's devastating and far-reaching effect on our world, we all find ourselves at times fogged in with blinding distortions about work. But we don't have to live in the fog. There is good news about our work that gives us hope amid the many distortions of work and the painful difficulty in that work.

Hopeful Realism in Our Work

In his bestseller *Good to Great*, Jim Collins recounts the story of his interaction with Admiral James Stockdale, who as a young man spent several years as a prisoner of war in what was dubbed the Hanoi Hilton. When Collins asked him about the difference between those prisoners who lost hope and gave up and those who endured such a torturous existence, Admiral Stockdale was quick to reply. The difference, he pointed out, was a kind of hopeful realism. The idealistic prisoners who convinced themselves they would be home by Christmas simply caved when Christmas after Christmas came and went. But the prisoners who prepared themselves for the likelihood of a long and difficult captivity and yet believed they would eventually triumph and make it back home were the ones who fared better and ultimately survived.[6]

If we are going to survive a lifetime of work in a fallen world, we need to cultivate a hopeful realism. Our minds may be filled with idealistic phantoms of the perfect dream job or career. It is easy to be set up for disappointment when we hear things like, "Do what you love to do, and you will not work a day in your life." While some of us may get to do work we love to do and get paid for it, many others do not. Many faithful followers of Jesus do not have a great deal of choice when it comes to their jobs. Sometimes, bills just need to be paid. Even if we truly enjoy our work, there are parts of it we do not like and difficult people we encounter. Sometimes we face fierce storms and need to be resilient. International pop star Taylor Swift has learned how to stay agile and turn many obstacles into opportunities. She offers this helpful perspective: "Life isn't how you survive the storm, it's about how you dance in the rain."[7] No matter your present circumstances, you can remain resilient and hopeful. You can dance in the rain.

God has really good news for you and your work: work can be redeemed. With adjusted expectations and a hopeful realism, you can confidently face the broken Babel workplaces that greet you in your Monday world. Though sin and death entered the world in a garden long ago, the good news is Jesus came to this broken planet. Through his death and resurrection, Jesus is the redeemer not only of human souls but of the whole world. Because of what he has done for you, you can now experience a life with God as you work with God for his glory in his kingdom. This good news of redemption is where we turn our attention next in God's work story.

A Prayer for Our Work

Almighty God, by whose will we were created, and by whose providence we have been sustained, grant to us your blessing this day. You have given to each of us our work in life; Lord, enable us to diligently perform our respective duties. May we not waste our time in unprofitableness and idleness, nor be unfaithful to any trust committed to us. By Your grace strengthen each of us for the performance of duties before us.[8]

Questions for Reflection and Discussion

- How have you experienced the brokenness of work in a fallen world?
- How does recognizing the brokenness of work change the way you view your work and workplace?
- Which distortion of work is most apparent in your workplace?
- Which distortion of work do you most easily fall into?
- Knowing more of God's story of work, how might you cultivate a more hopeful realism in your workplace?

3

Work's Gospel Transformation

The first Adam was cursed with labor and suffering; the redemption of labor and suffering is the triumph of the second Adam—the Carpenter nailed to the cross.

—Dorothy Sayers[1]

I remember the first time I met Ron for lunch. Although Ron had not gone to church for a long time, he had recently been attending our Sunday morning worship services, and to his surprise he had found his church experience meaningful. Ron had a lot of questions about the Christian faith. At first glance, he displayed the many appealing attributes of a successful career in sales and marketing. He was warm, engaging, and confident. His years of work had honed his social and relational skills to a razor-sharp competency, but as we talked further Ron revealed more about the currents swirling underneath.

Ron had two failed marriages and a growing sense of discontentment in the corporate world. He wanted to know what the Christian faith was and how it connected to his messy life and highly competitive work environment. Over the next couple of months, Ron and I met several times, and I shared with him the gospel, what Jesus taught, what he had done, and what he offers to those who would embrace and follow him. We had a thoughtful conversation about how the good news of Jesus transforms us from the inside out. We discussed how it reshapes how we view the world as well as how we live and work. We talked extensively about how the Christian faith permeates all of life and seamlessly connects what we profess to believe on Sunday and how we practice our work on Monday.

Ron was pleasantly surprised as he began to grasp that his trust in Jesus saves him not only *from* sin but also *for* a redeemed life of purpose. The good news of Jesus offers a new life entirely, bringing new purpose and meaning as well as an integral coherence to all of life. The gospel answers the big why question and makes sense of life. I will never forget the look of joy in Ron's eyes as he contemplated the truth that the Christian faith is not about being good enough to somehow be accepted by God. Throughout his life Ron had thought that the main message of Christianity was about being good enough for God to let a person into heaven. Now Ron realized that the gospel called him to place his complete trust in Jesus, that he couldn't earn a right standing before a holy God, and that salvation was a gift he was to receive in repentance and faith.

Over the weeks and months that followed, I saw the transforming power of the gospel in Ron's life. His love for Christ and the fruit of the Spirit became increasingly evident. Ron's commitment to his marriage strengthened. Though the day-to-day challenges of his workplace did not immediately change, Ron's attitude toward his work did so—profoundly. He embraced his work with a renewed passion, empowerment, and creativity. Because things were going well in his soul, Ron was more focused at work. He brought a new calm and confidence to the workplace. He viewed his coworkers through the loving lens of grace, affirming them and seeking their success and betterment. The good news of Jesus not only made Ron a more integrated person; it also made him a much better boss and employee.

Ron's story reminds us that God's work story is not just about the brokenness we endure in our Monday worlds but also about the real change and hopeful transformation we experience there. God's work story is about transforming work from what it now is to what it can be, one worker at a time.

Redemptive Work in the Old Testament

As we consider God's work in the first chapters of the Old Testament, we see stories of God bringing his redemption to the work of ordinary people. These stories foreshadow the pinnacle of God's redemptive work in Jesus Christ, the great savior of our souls and our work.

Consider the story of Joseph, who faces unimaginable injustice and exploitation from his family yet continues to be faithful to God. In Egypt, he works diligently as the manager of Potiphar's household and even remains faithful to God when he is unjustly put in prison. Then in Pharaoh's court, God honors Joseph and he becomes the second-highest leader in the greatest superpower in the world. Joseph's wise and excellent work saves a nation from famine and moves God's mission forward. His success came from aligning himself with God's agenda. He therefore experienced God's best for his work, even within a very broken environment. Joseph's story reminds us of God's redemption of our individual lives and our workplaces. God can redeem even the difficulties, frustrations, and sufferings. He can take the junk from our work and turn it into art. He can bring order to chaotic things; he can bring dead things back to life.

It is not incidental that God first appears to Moses in his workplace in the pastureland of Midian. Moses, as a working shepherd, is told to lead God's people out of Egypt to the promised land.

As Moses's story continues, his faithfulness in his everyday work was God's unique way of preparing him for the tasks ahead. God's presence at the burning bush was to accompany him in all his endeavors. Moses's life reminds us that when we look to God for our energy and strength, we operate within his power to accomplish good things in our work.

If we're asked to name other biblical characters, Bezalel and Oholiab are typically not the first who come to mind. Even for a seasoned student of the Bible they are tough to recall and even more difficult to pronounce. Though Bezalel and Oholiab would be excellent candidates for a difficult Bible trivia question, their lives and vocational calling were anything but trivial. They were part of Israel when Moses received the Ten Commandments on Mount Sinai. These "Ten Words," as they were labeled in the original Hebrew language, were written on two stone tablets and codified God's moral law. They also laid out God's boundaries for human flourishing.

In addition to the Ten Commandments, God gave Moses extensive instructions on how he desired to be worshiped. At this time in redemptive history, God instructed his covenant people to offer blood sacrifices for their sin in a tabernacle that involved various instruments of worship such as altars and basins. This is where Bezalel and Oholiab found their vocational calling as artisan craftsmen. In Exodus 31 we read, "The LORD said to Moses, 'See, I have called by name Bezalel the son of Uri, son of Hur, of the tribe of Judah, and I have filled him with the Spirit of God, with ability and intelligence, with knowledge and all craftsmanship, to devise artistic designs, to work in gold, silver, and bronze, in cutting stones for setting, and in carving wood, to work in every craft. And behold, I have appointed with him Oholiab, the son of Ahisamach, of the tribe of Dan. And I have given to all able men ability, that they may make all that I have commanded you'" (vv. 1–6 ESV). In giving Moses such a detailed work order, God had been preparing and gifting workers who could accomplish the task at hand.

There is much to glean from this passage from Exodus. We read, "See, I have called by name Bezalel" (31:2 ESV). In the original language of the Old Testament, the name Bezalel means "In the shadow (protection) of God." Though Bezalel might seem to us like an obscure character, his name tells us that he is anything but obscure in God's eyes. God calls Bezalel by name, and his word to Moses affirms three big ideas. First, Bezalel's vocational call was observed by others around him. Second, his calling was specific to him as an individual. Third, God supernaturally empowered and gifted Bezalel for a specific work, a vital contribution to God's redemptive program.

The first person filled with the Holy Spirit in the Old Testament is a worker. It is said of Bezalel that he is filled with "the Spirit of God." This is the same language found in Genesis 1, where the Spirit of God moves over the original creation (Gen. 1:2). Christian theologians understand this as a trinitarian reference to the Holy Spirit. In Exodus 31, the biblical author validates the Holy Spirit's supernatural filling work in and through observable external evidence—namely, Bezalel's vocation. Four qualities are carefully strung together to present a compelling picture of Bezalel's empowerment and gifting: the Spirit of God had filled Bezalel with "ability and intelligence, with knowledge and all craftsmanship" (v. 3).

The text doesn't indicate that Bezalel was suddenly granted instant artistic ability; his craftsmanship had been honed through years of diligent learning and practical experience. Like all skilled workmen, Bezalel had learned from craftsmen who had gone before him. However, the biblical writer has more than attained human competence in mind. He wants us to know the Spirit of God had gifted Bezalel for his particular vocational calling. God had supernaturally empowered Bezalel as a gifted architect, craftsman, and builder. The beauty and excellence of his work inspired awe. This was true not only of the excellent artistry and craftsmanship of Bezalel and Oholiab; we are told that God gave "to all able men ability" in making the wilderness tabernacle (Exod. 31:6 ESV). These weighty words have profound implications for our lives and our world. Our vocational callings are woven into the beautiful tapestry of God's mysterious providence. Through the eyes of faith, we can be confident that God is moving his redemptive story forward and empowering us to participate with him and his work in the world. You were created with work in mind. You have been gifted to do particular work. The Holy Spirit has equipped, gifted, and empowered you, as a follower of Christ, for a vocational contribution that God has providentially arranged for you to make in this world.

David Greusel is a modern-day Bezalel. Due to his quiet and unassuming manner, you might not guess he is a world-class architect who has designed stadiums and convention centers around the globe. David, like most followers of Jesus, has wrestled with what Sunday faith means for work every other day of the week. He has sought to find his God-honoring vocational contribution to the world. He has thought deeply about work and its important implications for a life of Christian faithfulness, human flourishing, and the common good.

As David tells the story, the example of Bezalel proved transformative in his spiritual journey and gave him the green light to pursue architecture. As David penned in an email, "Exodus 31 has been so important to me in understanding the work that I do as God-given and Spirit-filled. This is such a huge insight that I feel the church has overlooked for years when it has had on its institutional blinders—blinders that only 'church work' can be Spirit-led or Spirit-filled." For David, living a Spirit-filled life is embedded in a robust theology of vocation in which his Christian faith is increasingly and seamlessly woven into all facets of life. As an apprentice of Jesus, David has a clear sense of his vocational calling. His work has become his primary place of discipleship as well as how he brings truth, goodness, and beauty to the world. He and all the hands that build a sturdy stadium serve the common good by bringing a diverse city together. Even in the midst of a broken workplace, David is an agent of redemption, exuding a disciplined diligence and finding confidence, creativity, and contentment as he relies on a supernatural empowerment to work as an architect.

Jesus, Our Transforming Redeemer

God's unfolding story of work tells us real change is possible in our lives and our work. Embedded in Genesis 3 is a prophetic hint of God's plan for redeeming fallen creation and fallen work: the serpent who had brought sin, disintegration, and death into God's good world would one day be crushed.[2] As the biblical story unfolds, we encounter God's plan of making things right again. His sovereign plan of restoration and redemption is now on the march in history. The late pastor Timothy Keller articulates well the big picture of God's good news story: "The gospel is the true story that God made a good world that was marred by sin and evil, but through Jesus Christ he redeemed it at infinite cost to himself, so that someday he will return to renew all creation; end all suffering and death; and restore absolute peace, justice, and joy in the world forever."[3] This long-awaited redeemer would one day come to earth as an anointed one, a Messiah, who would shatter the curse unleashed on creation and set us and the world right again.

In the Gospel of John, we encounter Jesus, the eternal Son of God, the Word, who takes on human flesh, becoming one of us, coming into the world to redeem us.[4] John reminds us that this Jesus who arrived on a sin-scarred planet is the very one present and active at creation. John says of Jesus, "All things were created through him, and apart from him not one thing was created that has been created" (John 1:3). As John's Gospel unfolds, we see that the work of God in creation continues through the work of Jesus—a work of new creation that brings total transformation.

In Jesus's public appearance to Israel, he came with one central message: "Repent, for the kingdom of heaven is at hand" (Matt. 3:2; 4:17 ESV). The kingdom of God—or we might call it the all-encompassing reign of God, which is from everlasting to everlasting—is now available to anyone who will trust in Jesus. This trust in the King and his kingdom involves every dimension of our lives, including our work.

45

This kingdom is not a thin religious or ethical veneer but rather goes to the core of our minds and hearts. When we embrace the good news, we move from spiritual death to spiritual life. We are transformed from the inside out. In John 3, Jesus describes this core gospel transformation as a spiritual birth to a first-century religious leader by the name of Nicodemus. When we trust Jesus, we experience a new birth. Paul describes this spiritual birth using new creation language: "Therefore, if anyone is in Christ, he is a new creation, the old has passed away, and see, the new has come!" (2 Cor. 5:17). Creation is not just something God did long ago in bringing the world into existence; he is still creating through the transforming power of the gospel and the supernatural work of the Holy Spirit.

When we embrace and follow Jesus as our personal Lord and Savior, we are given a new identity. We are now God's beloved children, adopted into his family, ushered into his kingdom reign. As important as our work is, when we experience this love, we no longer look to our work to provide our ultimate security or significance. Keller describes well how the gospel transforms our understanding of work as we now see both ourselves and others differently: "The gospel frees us from the relentless pressure of having to prove ourselves and secure our identity through work, for we are already proven and secure. It also frees us from a condescending attitude toward less sophisticated labor and from envy over more exalted work. All work now becomes a way to love the God who saved us freely; and by extension, a way to love our neighbor."[5]

The Prodigal Sons

In the Gospel of Luke, Jesus tells a story about a runaway son. Before running off to a far country, this prodigal son did the unthinkable, disgracing his family and demanding from his father his share of the family inheritance. The father granted his son's wish. Off the young man went, embracing a slothful, self-indulgent, immoral lifestyle. Over time, he squandered all that his father had worked for. Hitting rock bottom, the son made his way back to his father's loving arms. His father threw a party for him and with lavish grace received him back into the family. But before we celebrate the return of the prodigal, we should remember that Jesus's good news story doesn't end here. There is another son in Jesus's story: Whereas the younger son was slothful, the elder son was a hard worker at home. And *both* sons were estranged from their loving father.

The elder brother stayed at home, followed the rules, and dutifully worked hard. Though he had not physically left home, the elder brother had left his father's heart. None of his hard work was the fruit of a loving relationship with his father. The tragedy of Jesus's good news story is that while the younger brother was lost and then found, the elder brother neither realized nor admitted that he was lost—and we are left not knowing if he was ever found. As Keller notes, "Jesus the storyteller deliberately leaves the elder brother in his alienated state. The bad son enters the father's feast but the good son will not. The lover of prostitutes is saved, but the man of moral rectitude is still lost."[6] Without flowing from a relationship with the Father, hard work, however noble, proves to be empty. The elder brother was working only for himself.

What a pitiful and tragic aim. The work we do will not win us favor with the Father. Yet as new creations in Christ, transformed from the inside out, we are once again able to do the work we were created for.

Jesus's Death and Resurrection

At the center of this work of new creation is Christ's cross and resurrection. In a tragic moment of perverted justice, human religious and political power came together to slander and condemn to death the author of life. The perfect Son of God walked fully in his Father's will, which led him to great suffering at the hands of evil. In his death, he experienced far more deeply than we can ever know the pain we experience in our working world. He experienced psychological humiliation, physical torture, and the weight of the sin and shame of the whole world.

The cross of Jesus is both hideous in its cruel injustice as well as glorious in its sacrificial love. The apostle Paul reminds us of this when he says, "But God shows his love for us in that while we were still sinners, Christ died for us" (Rom. 5:8 ESV). On the cross, the one true triune God paid the ultimate price and provided the ultimate swap for your sin and mine. As Paul says, "For our sake he [God the Father] made him [God the Son] to be sin who knew no sin, so that in him [Jesus] we might become the righteousness of God" (2 Cor. 5:21 ESV). Jesus's atoning death on the cross was not the end, though. He burst forth in glory after three days, so that death is no longer the final word for humanity or for our work. Collaboration with the risen Jesus in our work is still possible today. Our greatest opportunity is to become his students, his disciples, learning to live life and do our work in his kingdom. Our hearts, lives, and work will be transformed if we put our trust in the risen Jesus, embrace his agenda for our lives, and come under his tutelage by embracing him as Savior, Lord, and Teacher.

When we embrace Jesus and follow him, our true north moves from accomplishment for him to intimacy with him. Trusting that Jesus delights in us, we become free to pursue intimacy with him at work, bringing a Christlike presence and virtuous goodness in our broken workplaces. The apostle Peter captures this transformation that empowers us in our Monday worlds: "His divine power has given us everything required for life and godliness through the knowledge of him who called us by his own glory and goodness" (2 Pet. 1:3).

A Transformed Worker

His name meant "useful," but he proved himself anything but useful to his boss. As an indentured household servant in the first century, Onesimus's work likely wasn't all that appealing. The long hours and endless domestic duties must have seemed mundane and meaningless. Perhaps Onesimus had long thought about leaving his post, or maybe a particular dehumanizing or painful incident was the straw that broke the camel's back. What prompted Onesimus to leave remains a mystery, but one day he left his boss and work behind and bolted to the big city of Rome.

While in Rome, something unexpected happened that changed Onesimus forever: Paul shared with him the good news of the gospel. Onesimus encountered the crucified and resurrected Christ and experienced transforming grace. For the first time in his life, Onesimus was truly free. Yet he still had a job to do. We know this from an inspired letter that made its way into the New Testament and named for its recipient, Onesimus's boss, Philemon.

Paul sends Onesimus back to Philemon with a letter in hand that urges him to receive his household servant and put him back to work. Paul writes, "I appeal to you for my child, Onesimus, whose father I became in my imprisonment. (Formerly he was useless to you, but now he is indeed useful to you and to me)" (Philem. 10–11 ESV). Paul's heartfelt appeal is not based on giving his household servant a humanitarian or altruistic second chance (however noble that might have been) but rather on the power of the gospel to transform lives. Paul's letter informs us that Philemon himself had experienced the power of the gospel. With this in mind, Paul urges Philemon to receive Onesimus back not only as a household servant but more importantly as a new brother in Christ. Philemon is to view Onesimus not merely as a worker but rather as a worker created in the image of God, whose identity is now centered in Christ. As Paul sends Onesimus back to Philemon, he sends him back as a worker—one transformed by Jesus Christ.

Audience of One

One of my first jobs was working in the fast-food industry, which often involves long hours, particularly on the weekends, and is often underappreciated, causing high turnover. Shortly after I began working, I noticed that many of my coworkers acted differently when our manager was absent. They did not work as hard, took longer breaks than they were supposed to, and cut corners in just about any way you can imagine. I also noticed my fellow employees who were Christians behaved and worked consistently whether the boss was present or not. I didn't know it at the time, but I soon learned that it was not merely a strong work ethic but rather clarity about who they were ultimately working for. There was another boss in the picture.

Paul encourages first-century Christians to be diligent in their work, reminding them of their audience of one: "Don't work only while being watched, as people-pleasers, but work wholeheartedly, fearing the Lord. Whatever you do, do it from the heart, as something done for the Lord and not for people, knowing that you will receive the reward of an inheritance from the Lord. You serve the Lord Christ" (Col. 3:22–24).

The gospel not only changes our hearts and how we view the world; it also changes who we ultimately work for, and this transforms us and the work we do. Few truths will change your life and your work more than remembering your audience. It may not always feel this way, but everywhere we are, including our workplaces, is holy ground because God is there. Like Moses, we, too, can encounter burning bushes in our workplaces, yet we may miss them if we're not attentive. A helpful practice is to put small reminders of your audience of one in your workplace. You may want to put "audience of one" on your phone, your computer screen, or some visible place where you work. This small discipline helps me not forget that God is present with me and that he is the one I am ultimately working for. Working before an audience of one puts me in a posture of worship, reminds me of God's presence, and encourages greater diligence in my daily work.

Salt and Light at Work

In his Sermon on the Mount, Jesus employs the metaphors of salt and light to communicate the influence people transformed by the gospel bring to the world. Speaking to his followers, Jesus proclaims, "You are the light of the world. A city set on a hill cannot be hidden. Nor do people light a lamp and put it under a basket, but on a stand, and it gives light to all in the house. In the same way, let your light shine before others, so that they may see your good works and give glory to your Father who is in heaven" (Matt. 5:14–16 ESV). In all aspects of our lives, including our workplaces, we display to those around us the light of the glory of Christ indwelling us. Jesus emphasizes that we shine his light in our good works, and that includes our daily work.

One of the most important ways we act as redemptive agents in this broken world is by maintaining a faithful presence in the workplace. Think about how many hours a week are devoted to your work. It's estimated we spend around one hundred thousand hours of our life in work-related activities.[7] Both paid and unpaid work make up a huge chunk of our lives. Remember, God designed it that way. We do not simply work to live; in many ways we live to work. Sociologist James Davison Hunter has thought a great deal about cultural change and Christian faithfulness in the modern world. Hunter reminds us that first and foremost Christ is faithfully present to us. Because Christ is faithful to us, we are to be faithful to others: "Faithful presence in the world means that Christians are fully present and committed in their spheres of influence, whatever they may be: their families, neighborhoods, voluntary activities and places of work."[8] When we are faithfully present we form and deepen relationships by demonstrating a willingness to receive others as Christ would receive them, with gentleness, kindness, and humility. Another important part of faithful presence is doing consistent and excellent work. Faithful presence does not mean we will always stay in the same job; rather, we commit to being "fully there" wherever we are while we are there. As followers of Jesus we are called to a mission of engagement in the broader world. Faithfully engaging the world means being fully present as we embrace our vocations.

Vocation is a vital concept in the Christian story. My friend Steve Garber asserts that vocation is not incidental but rather integral to the mission of God in the world.[9] What does vocation mean? Vocation means "calling" and reminds us that we have a caller, God himself, who draws us into an intimate relationship with himself. Our primary calling or vocation is to someone, not to something.

But we have other important secondary callings in both our relationships and our work. A large part of stewarding our vocational callings in the workplace is faithfully showing up every day and living out the gospel by doing good work and being exemplary workers. It means we extend grace to our coworkers and our customers and seek their good. As image bearers of God, who is a worker, our work has intrinsic value in itself and is an act of worship. Also, our work has instrumental value in that it provides for the needs of ourselves and others. Furthermore, it creates a sphere of influence for the gospel to be lived out and shared as we embody a faithful presence in the world.

Demi Lloyd serves as CEO of DEMDACO, a design-driven company located in Kansas City specializing in gifts and home decor. God's story of work has not only transformed Demi's workplace behavior and values; it has also shaped DEMDACO's culture through the broad redemptive implications of the gospel. DEMDACO is not a Christian company, but, called by God to be a business leader, Demi is committed to modeling a faithful presence in the workplace.

Many of Demi's colleagues do not profess Christian faith, and some do not profess any faith at all, but DEMDACO is intentional about nurturing a corporate culture that holds high the value of each person, the value of work, and the importance of seeking the common good and of being a redemptive influence. A relentless commitment to pursue work as it ought to be reflects the biblical storyline of work and makes its way into the very purpose of the company. DEMDACO's stated purpose is "to lift the spirit by providing products that help people connect in a meaningful way and by pursuing business as it ought to be."[10] Demi not only is a cherished friend but also has modeled for me and so many others the multifaceted influence that the gospel has on us as workers, the work we do, and our workplaces.

Jesus said that he came to give us abundant life. While this life is eternal, it also permeates our daily work. Jesus invites you to embrace him as your personal Lord and Savior. We embrace Jesus in a spirit of repentance for our sin and place our complete trust in him. We cannot earn Jesus's love or acceptance by trying to be good enough or religious enough. His invitation to you is one of grace, of unmerited favor. If you have not yet embraced Jesus as your personal Lord and Savior, let me encourage you to pause right here and in honest prayer reach out to him. He is there for you, waiting for you, and longs to give you the life you were created to live.

Jesus is the author of the good news story. He enters into the story and extends an invitation to you. Without knowing Christ, you and I will never experience the life for which we were created. Without knowing Christ, your work will never be all that God intended it to be. Without knowing the one who created work in the first place, your work will never be ultimately fulfilling. Express your complete trust in him not only to forgive you but to give you the life God has always intended you to have. The good news of work is that we as broken image bearers of God can be transformed, that our world of work and the workplaces we spend so much time in can be transformed. And one day work will be all it was designed to be. The glorious future of our work is where we turn our attention to next.

A Prayer of Thanks

Heavenly Father, we thank you for the glorious good news. May the rich truths of the gospel press more deeply into who we are and the work we are called to do. Holy Spirit, guide and empower us to live the new life you have called us to live.

Questions for Reflection and Discussion

- How does understanding what work can be in light of the good news change the way you view your work and your workplace?
- How is the good news transforming the way you work?
- How can working before an audience of one shape the way you work?
- Are you being salt and light in your workplace? Does the work you are doing point others to God?
- What does being a faithful presence mean for your Monday?

4

Work's Grand Future

The created order, which God has begun to redeem in the resurrection of Jesus, is a world in which heaven and earth are designed not to be separated but to come together. In that coming together, the "very good" that God spoke over creation at the beginning will be enhanced, not abolished.

—N. T. Wright[1]

Greensburg, Kansas, was once only known as home of the world's largest hand-dug well. But that all changed on the evening of May 4, 2007.[2] At 9:25 p.m. tornado sirens alerted the sleepy town of 1,500 residents that trouble was on its way. Folks rushed to their storm shelters and basements as the 205-mile-per-hour winds of an F5 tornado reduced their town to piles of rubble. In the course of a few minutes, the fast-moving twister laid down a destructive path twenty-two miles long and almost two miles wide.

The aftermath of the tornado is hard to describe. Greensburg looked as if a megaton bomb had been dropped on it. Ninety-five percent of the town was destroyed. Eleven residents lost their lives.

The entire town was homeless. All businesses and social services were gone. This historic and quintessential Midwestern town had been completely wiped off the map.

But the Greensburg community never lost hope in a better future. Cleanup began almost immediately. In some ways the architecture of the new Greensburg would reflect its past, but in other ways it would be vastly different. A bold plan to create a more environmentally conscious and sustainable Greensburg was conceived. The city council passed a resolution stating that all city buildings were to be built to the highest green standards, making it the first city in the nation to do so. Powered by wind turbines, Greensburg would be rebuilt as a "green" town. A nonprofit called GreenTown was formed to help residents embrace and implement the community's new green-living initiative. Though once devastated by a killer tornado, Greensburg, Kansas, is back on the map.

God's work story is a storyline of redemptive work in our broken world. The Bible places human work within the broader theological framework of God's unfolding redemption of all things. God created a good world where our work was in harmony with his design. But because of sin and death, God's good world was ravaged and our good work was devastated—a killer F5 twister that left a path of destruction altering the topography of us workers and our work.

Yet there is good news for us and our work both now and in the future. A loving God conceived and implemented a plan of redeeming us workers and our work when he sent his Son to this sin-scarred planet. In and through the glorious gospel, our gracious Lord and Savior calls us to himself, to know him and be known by him. Jesus invites us to join him in his loving, grand, and glorious restoration and rebuilding project. Jesus's kingdom is on the move and is building toward a grand finale. Jesus's redemptive enterprise is in one sense already occurring, but in another sense it is not fully accomplished. We live and work in an already-but-not-yet moment of redemptive history. In a time between what *can* be and what *will* be, we work with new empowerment, motivated by love with a renewed sense of significance and growing anticipation of what lies ahead.

In this between time, we not only have the promise of eternal life in the future; we have eternal life here and now. Jesus frames eternal life not merely within the time constructs of a future reality but within a never-ending relationship with himself that is available to us now. In his high priestly intercession, Jesus prays, "This is eternal life: that they may know you, the only true God, and the one you have sent—Jesus Christ" (John 17:3). When we know Jesus in this way, our lives and work reflect their original design. In the power of the Holy Spirit, we are empowered to exercise a redemptive influence on our work, our fellow workers, and our workplaces as we look to Christ and to a glorious future.

In your day-to-day vocation, remember that, while your work will not be all it was intended to be in this fallen world, a new and better world of work is coming. One day your labor will be as God designed it to be in a pristine garden long ago. Your work in the new creation will be even better than it was in the original creation. God has great things in store for his image-bearing workers, and how you work matters for the future as well as the present.

We are often curious about the future, and Jesus's first-century disciples were no exception. Steeped in the Old Testament Scriptures, the disciples understood that history was not a series of meaningless, random events. They believed history was being skillfully guided by the hand of a good and sovereign God. History was moving somewhere, but where? How would the future unfold? What might that mean for the present? Overcome by curiosity, the New Testament writer Matthew tells us, the disciples ask Jesus about the future.

Jesus Tells a Work Story

Responding to his disciples, Jesus paints a compelling picture of unfolding future events and the restoration of all things. His aim is not to give every detail but rather to urge the disciples to live with discernment and expectancy, always being prepared for his return to this earth. To drive home his point, Jesus tells a story about work, often referred to as the parable of the talents. A parable is simply a story that communicates an important spiritual or ethical truth. Jesus sets this parable about the future in the context of the workplace. Matthew invites us to listen in on Jesus's story:

> For it is just like a man about to go on a journey. He called his own servants and entrusted his possessions to them. To one he gave five talents, to another two talents, and to another one talent, depending on each one's ability. Then he went on a journey. Immediately the man who had received five talents went, put them to work, and earned five more. In the same way the man with two earned two more. But the man who had received one talent went off, dug a hole in the ground, and hid his master's money.
>
> After a long time the master of those servants came and settled accounts with them. The man who had received five talents approached, presented five more talents, and said, "Master, you gave me five talents. See, I've earned five more talents."
>
> His master said to him, "Well done, good and faithful servant! You were faithful over a few things; I will put you in charge of many things. Share your master's joy."
>
> The man with two talents also approached. He said, "Master, you gave me two talents. See, I've earned two more talents."
>
> His master said to him, "Well done, good and faithful servant! You were faithful over a few things; I will put you in charge of many things. Share your master's joy."
>
> The man who had received one talent also approached and said, "Master, I know you. You're a harsh man, reaping where you haven't sown and gathering where you haven't scattered seed. So I was afraid and went off and hid your talent in the ground. See, you have what is yours."
>
> His master replied to him, "You evil, lazy servant! If you knew that I reap where I haven't sown and gather where I haven't scattered, then you should have deposited my money with the bankers,

and I would have received my money back with interest when I returned.

"So take the talent from him and give it to the one who has ten talents. For to everyone who has, more will be given, and he will have more than enough. But from the one who does not have, even what he has will be taken away from him. And throw this good-for-nothing servant into the outer darkness, where there will be weeping and gnashing of teeth." (Matt. 25:14–30)

Jesus introduces us to three workers. In modern parlance, we might think of them as investment portfolio managers whom the owner has charged with managing his wealth and expanding his net worth. Two of the three workers invest well. But one demonstrates irresponsibility and slothfulness. He does not invest the resources entrusted to him but in effect stuffs the owner's cash in his mattress.

The two portfolio managers who demonstrate diligence in their work not only receive great commendation but are promised greater responsibility and opportunity in their future work. The owner says to them, "You were faithful over a few things; I will put you in charge of many things." The clear implication is that the owner has more work and greater responsibility in mind for his faithful workers. The irresponsible, slothful worker, however, receives a heart-stopping rebuke. The portfolio that had been entrusted to him is taken away and given to another, and the slothful worker's future work is not greater responsibility and opportunity but rather a hellish destiny where there is "weeping" and "gnashing of teeth."

What is Jesus saying to us? In light of his future return to earth, Jesus calls all who would follow him to lives of gospel readiness, faithfulness, and diligence, including in the workplace. Jesus makes the important connection that faithfulness now, in this already-but-not-yet moment in redemptive history, will be rewarded. Jesus's clarion call to faithfulness is set in the context of both the present and future work God has in store.

Reimagining Heaven

Jesus's parable of the talents encourages us to integrate the faith we profess on Sunday with the work we do on Monday. Diligent stewardship of all that has been entrusted to us is an authenticating mark of any follower of Jesus and an essential component of a life well lived. The writer of Ecclesiastes concludes his quest for life's meaning with unavoidable accountability to God: "For God will bring every act to judgment, including every hidden thing, whether good or evil" (12:14). Each one of us will one day give a full accounting to God for our life. And since such a large proportion of our time is devoted to our work, much of our accounting before God will be answering for the stewardship of the paid and unpaid work we have been called to do. Our most important job review will be the one Jesus gives us as we stand before him.

In the parable of the talents, Jesus paints an enticing picture of a future that rewards diligence and faithfulness. First and foremost, our future reward involves joyful intimacy with God. We will "share our master's joy," and we will be given greater work to do. Yes, we will still work in the new creation. In many ways our work today is preparation and training for what we will do in eternity. Our work is also an important part of our spiritual formation in becoming the person God desires for us to be in the new heavens and new earth. Work done for the glory of God and the good of our neighbor matters for eternity's job description.

God's story of the future of work suggests to us that heaven is more than a place to eternally chill out. The common notion of heaven being a destination of unending leisure, of playing harps on fluffy clouds, needs some careful reconsideration. What will heaven be like? It will be a place of eternal rest, but will it be more?

As a kid, I was very curious about heaven. I was told that heaven was a place far away where loved ones who had died had gone and that I, too, would join them one day. I remember lying on the cool green grass in my backyard, watching the cumulus clouds float by.

As I stared upward into the endless blue sky, I wondered exactly where heaven was and what people did there. Since I loved ice cream with a passion, I found myself imagining heaven as a place where you could eat ice cream all the time. The ice cream would be the best and it would never run out. And guess what? You would never get full; you could just keep eating banana split after banana split and then start in on some other delicious ice-cream treat. My idea of heaven was a never-ending eating frenzy, devouring ice cream with reckless abandon.

As I got older my conception of heaven became less indulgent. I came to believe that my future home in heaven and my current home on this sin-scarred earth were universes apart. I thought the earth was merely my present home. I did not realize that it was to be my *future home* as well. I perceived Scripture to be teaching that heaven was in a far-off place and that this world we live in would one day be abolished, completely destroyed by fire. It was all going to burn. But was my understanding in line with what the Bible really taught? Was it in line with God's work story?

The apostle Peter devotes much of his epistles to talking about the future. Peering down the corridor of time, Peter describes a day of future judgment that he along with the Old Testament prophets refer to as the day of the Lord. Peter writes, "But the day of the Lord will come like a thief; on that day the heavens will pass away with a loud noise, the elements will burn and be dissolved, and the earth and the works on it will be disclosed" (2 Pet. 3:10). Many translations of this text end with the earth being "burned up." While this translation can be supported, this linguistic rendering tends to convey the idea of complete annihilation and destruction rather than purification and healing.

As he peers into the future, Peter doesn't see a complete discontinuity between the past and the future, an infinite chasm between the original creation and the new creation. Rather, the unfolding future will have a significant degree of continuity with the present earth. With hopefulness anchored firmly in the future promise of

God and in God's declaration that original creation was good, Peter writes, "But according to his promise we are waiting for new heavens and a new earth in which righteousness dwells" (2 Pet. 3:13 ESV).

Peter's point is that the present earth will be purified from the ravaging effects of sin. Just as fire purifies precious metals such as gold or silver, so will God's original creation be purified. Paul also saw the fire of future judgment through the lens of purification rather than annihilation. Writing to the church at Corinth, Paul applies the imagery of fiery judgment to individual human works done in the name of God. Paul writes, "Each one's work will become obvious. For the day will disclose it, because it will be revealed by fire; the fire will test the quality of each one's work" (1 Cor. 3:13).

The fiery future judgment of our world, as well as our individual work, suggests there will be a considerable carryover from God's original creation to his new creation of the new heavens and new earth. God's original creation will not be wasted—it will be purified. Theologian N. T. Wright emphasizes this continuity between God's original creation and the new creation: "The transition from the present world to the new one would be a matter not of destruction of the present space-time universe but of its radical healing."[3]

The beautiful restoration of Greensburg enabled its residents to live better than they lived before. Greensburg is a signpost to the comprehensive transformation that awaits us and our world. When we begin to grasp that the destiny of our work and our world is not complete annihilation but rather radical healing, it changes how we view our daily work. If we believe that the earth, everything about it, and everything we do on it is simply going to be abolished and disappear, it then follows that our work is virtually meaningless. Why then should we make a tasty meal, learn a new skill, run a business, write a piece of music, or design a building if everything will one day be consumed by fire? It would make sense to work only enough to survive and simply get by. But if our daily work done for the glory of God and the common good will in some way carry over to the new heavens and new earth, then our present work overflows with immeasurable value.

Goodbye to Lifeboat Theology

If we are going to fully embrace the work God has called us to do, then we will need to say goodbye to what Paul Marshall aptly describes as lifeboat theology, which views this world as if it were the *Titanic*.[4] God's good world has hit the iceberg of sin and is irrevocably doomed. It is time to abandon ship and get as many people in as many lifeboats as we can. In this theological perspective, God's plan of redemption is concerned only with the survival of his people. However noble and well-meaning our efforts to salvage God's creation may be, at the end of the day, our work only amounts to rearranging deck chairs on the *Titanic*.

Marshall wisely calls us to abandon an impoverished lifeboat theology for what he refers to as an ark theology. The Genesis writer tells of humankind's deep, dark plunge into sin. The corruption of God's good creation and the wickedness of sin were so unimaginably horrific that he seriously considered wiping out his creation completely. In Genesis 6 we read, "So the LORD said, 'I will blot out man whom I have created from the face of the land, man and animals and creeping things and birds of the heavens, for I am sorry that I have made them'" (v. 7 ESV). But rather than annihilating all he had made and starting over, God extends gracious favor to a man named Noah. God makes a covenant with Noah and commissions him to build an ark. Rather than blotting out all of creation, Noah and his family and a host of living creatures are rescued and preserved in the ark from the destruction of the flood. God remains committed to restoring the earth and continuing with his original creation. After Noah exits the ark, God makes a covenant with him promising to never destroy the earth with a flood again.

The story of Noah reminds us that God has not given up on his good world. In a burst of rapturous praise, the psalmist declares that the whole earth and everything in it belongs to the Lord (Ps. 24:1). God still loves his world. He will not give up on his creation. A glorious future awaits the earth. The nineteenth-century hymn-writer Maltbie Babcock beautifully captures this truth:

> This is my Father's world, O let me ne'er forget.
> That though the wrong seems oft so strong, God is the
>   ruler yet.
> This is my Father's world: the battle is not done;
> Jesus who died shall be satisfied, and earth and heaven
>   be one.[5]

The fallen world we inhabit is still our Father's world. C. S. Lewis speaks to God's new creation as not unmaking but remaking: "The old field of space, time, matter and the senses is to be weeded, dug, and sown for a new crop. We may be tired of that old field: God is not. . . . We live amid all the anomalies, inconveniences, hopes, and excitements of a house that is being rebuilt. Something is being pulled down and something going up in its place."[6] Does your daily work reflect that you and your work are part of God's redemptive rebuilding project? Do you grasp this world's destiny, and have you thought about your important place in it? Can you imagine what it will be like to work in a radically healed workplace, a sinless work environment with other sinless humans?

For now, we are called to work in a world that is not yet radically healed. Much of our daily work is caring for our Father's world and those who call it home. We make things. We fix things. We care for things. We serve others. What we do here is not a waste, nor is it a waste of time. Your skills and abilities will not be wasted; they will be utilized and further developed in the future work God has for you to do in the new heavens and new earth. Your time here in this fallen world is preparing you for an eternity of activity and creativity. Your work matters not only now but also for the future.

New Heavens and New Earth

Just prior to his death and resurrection, Jesus told his disciples that he was going away to prepare a place for them and that he would come again (John 14:1–3). What future place did Jesus have in mind? Dallas Willard stretches our imagination as to our future work: "Thus, we should not think of ourselves as destined to be celestial bureaucrats, involved eternally in celestial 'administrivia.' That would be only slightly better than being caught in an everlasting church service. No, we should think of our destiny as being absorbed in a tremendously creative team effort, with unimaginably splendid leadership, on an inconceivably vast plane of activity, with ever more comprehensive cycles of productivity and enjoyment. *This* is the 'eye hath not seen, neither ear heard' that lies before us in the prophetic vision (Isaiah 64:4)."[7]

As the Bible winds to a close, we are given a stunning glimpse of a future new heaven and new earth. In Revelation 19, we encounter a great homecoming. There is a grand wedding with a lavish and joyful marriage banquet. Revelation 21 unveils the new home for Jesus and his bride, the church. The apostle John writes, "Then I saw a new heaven and a new earth; for the first heaven and the first earth had passed away, and the sea was no more. I also saw the holy city, the new Jerusalem, coming down out of heaven from God, prepared like a bride adorned for her husband" (vv. 1–2).

John's vision of our future home reveals both a continuity with our present earthly home as well as a good deal of discontinuity. He describes a new earthly city that "comes down" out of heaven. He gives us the name of the city, the new Jerusalem. Throughout Revelation 21, John's language is very earthy. For example, the new Jerusalem is built with walls and gates made of "earthly" precious metals and jewels such as gold, jasper, and sapphire. Although this future home has a kind of earthiness, it is also very different from our present home. There is delightful and mysterious discontinuity. This new home will be a place with no more tears, death, crying, or pain. As God was with Adam and Eve in the garden before their rebellion against him, now God will be with his redeemed people in the new Jerusalem. John describes the dazzling beauty of this new city where light comes not from the sun but from God himself. John writes, "Night will be no more; people will not need the light of a lamp or the light of the sun, because the Lord God will give them light, and they will reign forever and ever" (Rev. 22:5). God's vision of working with redeemed humanity will not be thwarted.

Rather than thinking of heaven as something way out there, a completely foreign and different reality, the biblical writers present our heavenly home as something "closer" to our earthly home. Marshall points out the transforming significance of what the Bible teaches regarding our future destiny: "It is also an unbiblical idea that the earth doesn't matter because we are going to go to heaven when we die. The Bible teaches that there will be a 'new heaven and a new earth.' Our destiny is an earthly one: a new earth, an earth redeemed and transfigured. An earth reunited with heaven, but an earth, nevertheless."[8]

Work Is Not a Waste

Often I hear from people that their daily work seems so boring or is such a waste of time. I am not in any way minimizing the difficulties, frustrations, and mundane aspects of our work. But if we look through the lens of God's work story, our work (no matter what we have been called to do) is meaningful and significant.

God's story of work should unleash fresh perspective and renewed passion to our lives. How we show up at work, how we do what we do, is all a reflection of the kind of person we are becoming and where our future hope lies. In God's work story our vocational callings are rich with eternal meaning and significance. Our attitude toward work and those we work with is transformed. A new, loving creativity and diligence emerges in our workplaces. A sense of hopeful anticipation of a glorious future in the new heavens and new earth fills our souls. Reflecting on our future destiny, Timothy Keller brings some hopeful tailwinds of encouragement into our souls: "At the end of history, the whole earth has become the Garden of God again. Death and decay and suffering are gone. . . . Jesus will make the world our perfect home again. We will no longer be living 'east of Eden,' always wandering and never arriving. We will come, and the father will meet us and embrace us, and we will be brought into the feast."[9]

"Meet Me at Home"

Her name was Delight, and the day she died, the planet seemed to shift. On that blustery March day, death blew through our family and altered the landscape of our lives. As I watched my mom breathe her last breath, a host of thoughts bombarded my mind and a myriad of feelings suffocated my soul. Though she had lived a long and full life, her death and its profound implications were still hard for me to grapple with. "Meet me at home" were the last written words mom had left behind. Words scribbled on a crumpled piece of paper reflecting her hope of a glorious future reunion in our heavenly home.

My mom's Christian faith was the most important thing to her. As a single mother much of her life, she had worked very long and hard hours as both a teacher and a homemaker. My mom was bright, curious, and gifted in so many ways. Always the idealistic romantic, she was a poet, an artist with words. She excelled in the art of hospitality. Her kitchen was always open and her well-worn hands always eager and ready to serve what she described as a "home burnt" meal. Mom knew no strangers, she only met new friends. Her death was an immeasurable loss to many, and in those dark hours of personal grief it all seemed to me like such a colossal waste. All of her gifts, experiences, and talents seemed to be indifferently swallowed up in death.

At my mother's memorial service, many words were spoken, a fitting tribute for such a life well lived. Yet it was not what was said that parted the veil of grief for me as much as what was observed. At the front of the church sanctuary was not a coffin but a kitchen table—her kitchen table. Surrounding the kitchen table were the tools of food preparation and hospitality she was so skilled at using. Mom's kitchen things were a tribute to the past, but they were much more. They were a reminder of the glorious future of her resurrected body and her work in the new heaven and new earth, a future where I know my mother will hear the words that each one of us who have embraced Christ long to hear: "Well done, good and faithful servant! You were faithful over a few things; I will put you in charge of many things. Share your master's joy."

God has much work for my mom, for me, and for you to do in the new heavens and new earth. In his famous hymn "Amazing Grace," John Newton looked to the future and penned these words: "When we've been there ten thousand years / Bright shining as the sun, / We've no less days to sing God's praise / Than when we first begun."

In the new heaven and new earth, we will sing God's praises with our lips in our resurrected bodies. And as glorious as that will be, we will have the privilege to also sing God's praises with our work. For you have been created by a working God with work in mind. You have been created to work with God. Your work is anything but a waste. It matters now, and it matters for the future. Rudyard Kipling said it wondrously in his poem "L'Envoi":

> When Earth's last picture is painted and the tubes are
>   twisted and dried,
> When the oldest colors have faded, and the youngest critic
>   has died,
> We shall rest, and, faith, we shall need it—lie down for an
>   aeon or two,
> Till the Master of All Good Workmen shall put us to work
>   anew! . . .

And no one shall work for money, and no one shall work
    for fame.
But each for the joy of the working, and each, in his
    separate star,
Shall draw the Thing as he sees It for the God of Things as
    They Are.[10]

Having now explored God's work story—of what ought to be, of what is, of what can be, and of what will one day be—we now take a closer look at Jesus, who is the author of the story and who for a brief moment in time stepped into that story. Jesus and his world of work speak into and shape our daily work.

A Prayer of Gratitude

Heavenly Father, our hearts are overflowing with gratitude know-ing that the work you have called us to do matters for eternity. We are delighted to work with you now, and we long for the day when we will know you more intimately and work with you creatively with great joy forever.

Questions for Reflection and Discussion

- Do you see your daily work with an eternal vantage point in mind?
- How does a glimpse of the future, of living and working in the new heaven and new earth, motivate you to develop greater skills and competencies in and through your present work?
- How does gaining a greater understanding of the future reframe your perspective of your fellow workers and the work they do?

5

Jesus the Carpenter

If God came into the world, what would he be like? For the ancient Greeks, he might have been a philosopher-king. The ancient Romans might have looked for a just and noble states-man. But how does the God of the Hebrews come into the world? As a carpenter.

—Phillip Jensen[1]

I don't know why I didn't see it for so long, but one day as I was reading through the Gospel of Mark, I stumbled across a verse that stopped me dead in my tracks. Mark 6 tells us that Jesus, who was then an itinerant rabbi, returned to his hometown of Nazareth. The crowd listened to Jesus teach in the synagogue and was stunned by their hometown "boy" displaying such extraordinary wisdom. In their eyes, Jesus was first and foremost a carpenter from Nazareth. Mark records the hometown crowd exclaiming, "Is not this the carpenter, the son of Mary and brother of James and Joses and Judas and Simon? Are not his sisters here with us?" (6:3 ESV).

I began to reflect on the significance of Jesus spending so much of his time on earth working with his hands. Here was the Son of God, sent to earth on a redemptive mission of seeking and saving the lost, of proclaiming the gospel, yet he spent the majority of his years on earth making things in an obscure carpentry shop. We know from Luke's Gospel that even at age twelve, Jesus was demonstrating his rabbinical brilliance to the brightest and best in Jerusalem. How did Jesus's brilliance fit in with a carpentry career? At first glance this doesn't seem to be a strategic use of Jesus's extraordinary gifts or his important messianic mission. Why was it the Father's will for Jesus to spend so much time in the carpentry shop instead of proclaiming the gospel and healing the multitudes in the Palestinian countryside?

From beginning to end, God's story of work locates Jesus primarily as creator and redeemer but also as a Nazarene carpenter. The New Testament records Jesus spending only about three of his thirty-three years on earth as an itinerant rabbi, doing work comparable to a pastor or missionary. Speaking of Jesus as a carpenter, Dallas Willard brings a refreshing perspective:

> If he were to come today as he did then, he could carry out his mission through most any decent and useful occupation. He could be a clerk or accountant in a hardware store, a computer repairman, a banker, an editor, doctor, waiter, teacher, farmhand, lab technician, or construction worker. He could run a housecleaning service or repair automobiles.
>
> In other words, if he were to come today, he could very well do what you do. He could very well live in your apartment or house, hold down your job, have your education and life prospects, and live within your family, surroundings, and time. None of this would be the least hindrance to the eternal kind of life that was his by nature and becomes available to us through him.[2]

In the book *More Than a Carpenter*, Josh McDowell points out a great deal of convincing evidence that supports the deity of Jesus. Of course, this is essential to understanding his person and work.

Yet in no way should we conclude that because Jesus was infinitely more than a carpenter, his vocational calling to work as a carpenter was somehow unimportant or done out of mere economic necessity. The Son of God was much more, but not less, than a carpenter. And the incarnational pattern of Jesus's sinless earthly life speaks volumes about the importance of our day-to-day work.

It is truly stunning to contemplate that the one who called each star by name is the same one who was joyfully content to work with his hands, making useful farm implements and household furniture in an obscure carpentry shop. I imagine him whistling as he worked. Jesus's work life tells us that he did not think being a carpenter was somehow below him. The apostle Paul gives us a glorious description of this carpenter from Nazareth: "He is the image of the invisible God, the firstborn of all creation. For by him all things were created, in heaven and on earth, visible and invisible, whether thrones or dominions or rulers or authorities—all things were created through him and for him. And he is before all things, and in him all things hold together" (Col. 1:15–17 ESV).

The master craftsman of the universe spent a great deal of time during his thirty-three years on our planet crafting things with his hands. The one who had masterfully fashioned humans from the dust of the earth made chairs for people to sit on. No doubt Jesus had strong, callused hands from what we might think of today as blue-collar work. It is all too easy for us to overlook the fact that Jesus knew what it meant to get up and go to work every day. Jesus experienced both the exhilaration and exhaustion of putting in a hard day's work. He faced work and a workplace profoundly affected by sin. I am sure Jesus dealt with difficult and demanding people in the workplace. I am also confident that the sinless Son of Man not only modeled humility in the workplace but also maintained a teachable spirit, learning and working under Joseph, his human guardian father. I doubt if Joseph was the perfect boss. I have yet to meet a perfect boss, even when I look into my mirror each morning.

73

We are rightly in awe when Jesus, shockingly ignoring cultural convention, picks up a basin and towel and washes his disciples' dirty, stinky feet. Yet we tend to forget that Jesus had been modeling a basin and towel kind of servanthood in a carpentry shop for many years. Jesus's humble service in a Nazareth workshop was the training ground for that glorious display of servanthood in an upper room in Jerusalem.

Jesus would not have seen his carpentry work as mundane or meaningless, for it was the work his Father had called him to do. I am confident Jesus was a top-notch carpenter. Even before Jesus entered his itinerant rabbinical work, Matthew reminds his readers of the Father's good pleasure in his Son. Following Jesus's baptism, the Spirit of God descended as a dove, and a voice out of heaven declared, "This is my beloved Son, with whom I am well-pleased" (Matt. 3:17). The Father had many reasons to be well pleased, but one important aspect must have been Jesus's work as a carpenter. Theologian John Dyer describes Jesus's well-pleasing work this way: "Jesus's first job also fulfills the call to 'cultivate and keep the garden' from Genesis, meaning that Jesus was serving as a second Adam not only in his righteousness but also in his deeply human work of making. Jesus was not an abstract or idealized human but a real man in time and space, within a specific culture, doing real work with his hands and with the tools his earthly father passed down to him."[3]

Jesus's Great Invitation

When we embrace God's good news work story, we follow Jesus, who invites us to become his apprentice and learn from him a whole new way of living. Jesus says, "Come to me, all who labor and are heavy laden, and I will give you rest. Take my yoke upon you, and learn from me, for I am gentle and lowly in heart, and you will find rest for your souls. For my yoke is easy, and my burden is light" (Matt. 11:28–30 ESV). In this great invitation to be yoked with Master Jesus, we are invited to experience life as God originally intended in the garden of Eden, before sin and corruption entered the world. The path to rest, this life as God originally designed for us to live, is made possible because of Jesus's death on the cross and his bodily resurrection. It is found in Jesus's yoke of apprenticeship, as day by day we learn to live our new creation life of intimacy and obedience.

The rest Jesus offers doesn't mean kicking back in a recliner; rather, it is a joyous ease in our work as we wear the yoke that has been tailor-made just for us. When we take on the yoke of Christ, we press into God's creation design for our lives, and we learn how Jesus would live our lives if he were us. A vital part of learning from Jesus, of being yoked with him, is walking the path of vocational faithfulness. A large component of our apprenticeship with Jesus takes place in our work, but it is often the last place we think of as part of our discipleship journey. Under Jesus's yoke we not only learn from him but also work with him in our workplaces. With Jesus always with us, we are never alone with our computer at our desk or in business meetings or in preparing food for our families. Jesus teaches us not only how to live—to view our work differently—but also how to work.

When her father died, she said, "Daddy, I am going to make you proud." For Joy Dahl, that promise meant twenty years devoted to a successful career. At age thirty-three, she became CFO of a radio broadcasting company in New York. She had the many accoutrements of career achievement—a beautiful house, lots of money and prestige—but behind her successful look and sparkly smile was a deeply empty place. One day a coworker gave her a Christian book. Reading the book prompted Joy to go back to church. Though she was receptive to faith and considered herself a Christian, learning more about Jesus started to speak to her deepest longings in ways that surprised her. With tears flowing from her eyes and joy flooding her heart, Joy embraced Jesus as her personal Lord and Savior.

As she continued to mature spiritually, she wondered how her Christian faith should speak into her work. As she wrestled with this question, other followers of Jesus in the marketplace began to offer wisdom to guide her. Growing in her apprenticeship with Jesus, Joy experienced transformation in her life and marriage. Her desire now was to do something important for God; in her mind, that initially meant doing church work or some kind of Christian missions. But as she learned more about what the Bible taught, she began to see her work through the lens of God's work story, which opened her eyes and deeply resonated with her heart. Wanting to learn more, Joy pursued a seminary degree. Eventually she went on to get her doctorate, focusing on the integration of Christian faith and work. Joy is growing in her apprenticeship with Jesus and becoming a more compelling ambassador of his kingdom to those she works with and the organization she serves. She also is a national spokesperson for how Christian discipleship is profoundly lived out and shaped in the workplace.

Extraordinary Ordinary Work

Writing to the first-century followers of Jesus at Colossae, the apostle Paul places vocational discipleship at the heart of apprenticeship with Jesus and a life of God-honoring worship. Paul writes, "And whatever you do, in word or in deed, do everything in the name of the Lord Jesus, giving thanks to God the Father through him" (Col. 3:17). His understanding of discipleship is all-encompassing, informing and shaping every aspect of life. There is no place where God is off-limits or where Jesus is not present to guide and train us in the new creation life we now have in him and daily live in his kingdom.

Paul's mention of the name of the Lord may at first be confusing. Is Paul saying we need to verbalize Jesus's name everywhere we go? While a verbal witness is a vital part of our discipleship, Paul says that Jesus's lordship as creator and redeemer includes every square inch of the universe. When we do everything in the name of the Lord Jesus, it simply means that every dimension of human existence, all that we are and do, every relationship we have, is to be God-centered, God-focused, and God-glorifying, aligning with his kingdom. And so, as followers of Jesus, our lives and work are to be constant reflections of who we say we follow.

I once heard the story of an encounter the legendary Alexander the Great had with one of his soldiers, who was a pitiful sight. The soldier was dressed sloppily, seemed disheveled, and reeked of a long night of drinking and debauchery. When asked by his great military commander what his name was, the soldier replied, "Alexander, sir." Alexander the Great glared back at the solider and said, "Soldier, either change your name or change your behavior."

As followers of Jesus, we represent him to the world around us. The word "Christian" means "little Christ." Paul calls us ambassadors of Christ. Others see what we believe and who we follow not only by what we say but also by observing the kind of person we are becoming and the work we are doing. Like our Master Jesus, who modeled excellent carpentry work, by his grace we seek to exhibit Christlikeness in our words and attitudes. We seek to labor with diligence and excellence in whatever work God has called us to do. Martin Luther King Jr. captured the heart of apprenticeship to Jesus in Monday discipleship: "If it falls to your lot to be a street sweeper, sweep the streets like Michelangelo painted pictures, like Shakespeare wrote poetry, like Beethoven composed music; sweep streets so well that all the host of Heaven and earth will have to pause and say, 'Here lived a great street sweeper, who swept his job well.'"[4]

We are called to discipleship with Jesus in our paid and unpaid work. In our workplaces, Jesus invites us to work with him and to learn from him how to do our work, increasingly delighting in his presence, living each day before our audience of one. Jesus is truly the most brilliant person in your vocational field of work. Follow him. Learn to obey what he taught, live how he lived, and relate how he related to others. Delight in his presence, whether that is tinkering under the hood of a car, filing reports in your office, pulling weeds in your garden, serving in a soup kitchen, or changing the diapers on your newborn child. He is there with you and for you.

For most of us, the work we are called to do involves a good deal of what seems insignificant and mundane. In my pastoral calling, there is a lot of busywork that simply needs to get done. But these kinds of tasks and duties are not throwaway hours. Rather, they are defined by the Latin phrase *ora labora*, which simply means, "to work is to pray, to pray is to work." I remember hearing my mom sing hymns she loved or recite poetry that nourished her soul as she washed dishes. Some of our most God-honoring worship is not the songs we sing in church on Sunday but the joyful, ongoing conversation we have with God as we work in often unknown and unappreciated spaces of toil.

Our ordinary work life is designed by God to be filled with extraordinary meaning, purpose, satisfaction, and joy. As pointed out earlier, the Hebrew word *avodah* presents to us a holistic understanding of work and worship, thereby eliminating any compartmentalization of a worshipful life. We worship God in and through our work, and one of the primary ways we love our neighbor is in and through our vocation. In his Great Commandment, Jesus calls us to love the Lord our God with all our heart, soul, mind, and strength, and our neighbor as ourself. A proper understanding of Christian vocation puts flesh and feet on this commandment.

Recently I was the recipient of neighborly love expressed through vocation. On a flight from Kansas City to Los Angeles, many individuals knowingly or unknowingly honored the Great Commandment through their work. When I arrived at the airport, the baggage handlers assisted me with my luggage. At the gate, security personnel ensured my safety. Then a gate agent facilitated my getting on the plane. On the plane, the pilots charted the course and readied us for flight. A maintenance team filled the plane with jet fuel and fixed a broken plane toilet. Once we were in flight, a flight attendant brought me a cup of coffee. Through many individuals working not only for a paycheck but also on my and others' behalf, I arrived at my destination, ready for my meetings.

One of the primary ways we tangibly love our neighbors is to do excellent work in our various vocations. When we come to

understand God's work story, we see that vocation is closely connected with loving our neighbors. Your work is your specific and
invaluable contribution to God's ongoing creation and is an essential aspect of God's Great Commandment to love your neighbor as
yourself. Martin Luther reminds us that "God does not need our
good works, but our neighbor does."[5] God is very much at work in
our vocational calling. He is using it to love others, transform us,
and transform the world.

Smelling Good at Work

I love walking into a room that is adorned with flowers. A fresh
bouquet fills the air with an inviting aroma. Whether it is flowers or
someone's perfume, we are drawn to delightful fragrances. Perhaps
this is what the apostle Paul has in mind when he says apprentices of
Jesus give off the aroma of Christ, the fragrance of the knowledge of
Jesus everywhere we go. Every day, when you arrive at your workplace, you bring a fragrance with you. I am confident that others
around you are noticing what you are wearing at work. What are
those around you at work smelling? Is it drawing them to Jesus?

One of the ways we radiate Christlike fragrance is the attitude
we wear, the gentleness and kindness we emanate. Paul reminds us
that those who are indwelt and empowered by the Holy Spirit will
give off a fragrance of love, joy, peace, patience, kindness, goodness, faithfulness, gentleness, and self-control. Paul's inspired words
to the followers of Jesus at Thessalonica are especially helpful in
cultivating a Christlike attitude about work. After urging the Thes-
salonians to seek the common good of all, Paul lays out three attitudinal orientations that powerfully transform our workplaces.
Paul says, "Rejoice always, pray without ceasing, give thanks in all
circumstances; for this is the will of God in Christ Jesus for you"
(1 Thess. 5:16–18 ESV).

In these powerful verses, Paul encourages us to cultivate a daily
attitude of joy, prayer, and gratitude. Though our work can be very

frustrating at times, and though we often deal with some very difficult and demanding people, we are empowered by the Holy Spirit to
positively influence a workplace culture that better promotes human
flourishing, collaborative teamwork, and the common good. If we
will commit Paul's inspired words to memory, we can take them to
work with us. Perhaps write out his words and put them somewhere
in your work space as a reminder. In my workplace, I often review
these words of encouragement and make the necessary attitudinal
adjustments throughout my day.

I am also particularly encouraged by the hopeful and promising truth of Proverbs 16:3: "Commit your work to the LORD, and
your plans will be established" (ESV). When we live and work
before an audience of one as an apprentice of Jesus, we have nothing to fear, nothing to hide, and nothing to prove. We devote our
complete energy to loving others and doing good work. Having
an audience of one means we practice the presence of God as we
go about our day and enjoy an ongoing conversation with him in
our workplaces. As an overflow of our walk with Christ, we bring
a positive, joyful outlook to our daily work. Because of our faith
and our understanding of Christian vocation, we give a warm smile
to our coworkers, even those who at times rub us the wrong way.
We look for the good in others and celebrate others' achievements.
We express our appreciation through kind words and handwritten
notes. Our increasingly virtuous presence and joyful, hopeful, and
encouraging attitude are the sweet and distinct aroma of Christ to
those around us. Wherever God has called you on Monday, as an
apprentice of Jesus you can make a big difference in the lives of
others, your workplace culture, and God's kingdom.

Workplace Diligence

The first-century followers of Jesus in Thessalonica had been profoundly changed by the power of the gospel.[6] Having affirmed the
gospel's redeeming work in their lives, Paul exhorts these believers

regarding the gospel's implications of diligent work. Paul calls these Christ followers to live a life of faithfulness in their daily labors. He writes, "Aspire to live quietly, and to mind your own affairs, and to work with your hands, as we instructed you, so that you may walk properly before outsiders and be dependent on no one" (1 Thess. 4:11–12 ESV).

An essential aspect of presenting our Christian faith to our neighbors is through the responsible diligence we exhibit in our work. As a pastor, I all too often hear small business owners lament their experience working with or doing business deals with self-professing Christians. Sometimes the painful regret revolves around shoddy work, overpromising and not delivering, or not paying their bills on time. Many of us have known a boss, employee, or colleague who is quite vocal and visible about their Christian faith, but we have become disillusioned by their lack of diligence, competence, and gracious respect. When followers of Jesus embrace God's work story, they strive to do good work and to be the most honest and virtuous people to work with and do business with. The gospel alters our workplace ethics.

Paul also makes this point in his letter to the Ephesians, reminding them how the gospel is to change how they work: "Let the thief no longer steal. Instead, he is to do honest work with his own hands, so that he has something to share with anyone in need" (Eph. 4:28). When we embrace the good news of Jesus and his story of work, our workplace ethics change. For one thing, we do not steal. Workplace theft can take many forms, from property theft of inventory or goods, fudging expense reports, misstating quarterly sales results, and doing personal things on company time. Even if done remotely, our work calls for a high standard of diligence and ethics. As followers of Jesus we no longer take what is not ours to take; rather, we choose to work honestly and diligently so that the economic remuneration we receive for our work allows us the financial capacity to give generously. Our honest, ethical, and diligent work allows us to support our local church and other charities as well as care for the under-resourced in our communities. Our workplace ethics are a distinct and compelling witness of gospel plausibility to the world, pointing others to the God we love and serve, advancing his kingdom.

Sometimes I hear followers of Jesus say that they want to do kingdom work, by which they usually mean work done in a nonprofit rather than for-profit context. Yet this framing of kingdom work is impoverished. Both nonprofit and for-profit work can be kingdom-oriented. Kingdom work is far-reaching, encompassing a wide range of vocations and endeavors. *Ultimately, all work done for others and for God's glory and with his Spirit's empowerment is kingdom work.* When we work for the glory of God and the good of others, we answer Jesus's prayer for his kingdom to come on earth as it is in heaven. The Lord's Prayer is not just for your Sunday worship but also for your Monday worship. The Holy Spirit is always with us, praying with us, and helping us to pray (Rom. 8:26–27). Prayer is an essential way we colabor with God. Do we grasp that the work we are called to do in our careers is in part an answer to our Lord's prayer? Regularly reciting the Lord's Prayer in the workplace is a helpful practice to invite God's work in and through us as we do our work.

Our work is a small but not insignificant part of God's sovereign trajectory of the future redemption of all things. My friend Amy Sherman describes this good news of God's kingdom coming to earth in Jesus this way: "Jesus' work is not exclusively about our individual salvation, but about the cosmic redemption and renewal of *all* things. It is not just about our reconciliation to a holy God—though that is the beautiful center of it. It is also about our reconciliation with one another and with creation itself."[7] If we continually align our will and our ways with Jesus's in our workplaces, we are doing kingdom work.

Changing Our Workplace Paradigm

When we grasp the truth of God's work story, we see our work and workplaces through a vastly different lens. A friend often reminds me of how this paradigm shift changed his approach to work. Previously he had understood his primary goal as a CEO to be making a lot of money and then giving to charitable causes. As a generous person, he gave sizable amounts to missionaries and philanthropic causes. Though he continues to give generously, the game changer was when he began seeing his work as having intrinsic value, not merely instrumental value. He recognized his work as valuable in itself—God-honoring and good. Work has value beyond its economic benefits or its platform for Christian ministry. Of course, work's economic benefits and the nonprofit opportunities it provides are good things, but they are not work's main goal. The primary goal is worship through a lifestyle of God-honoring vocational faithfulness.

Similarly, John's story of transformation also highlights the big change in his Monday world. I met him at a favorite coffee shop. After ordering our lattes, we sat down, and he shared with me his story. John grew up in a Christian home and had gone to a Christian college, yet he had always struggled with how mundane and meaningless his work seemed. Hunkered at his desk, John's day consisted mostly in writing and answering email and processing loans for commercial and residential property. The Sunday messages he had heard were that committed Christians went into "full-time Christian work" as pastors, parachurch workers, or cross-cultural missionaries, so he had always felt tinge of guilt. What really seemed to matter most at his church were the Bible and people's eternal souls, while the rest of this world was going to eventually burn up in a future day of judgment.

John could still recall one particular message by an impassioned parachurch worker, imploring young leaders to join their organization rather than a business career, which would, in essence, be like rearranging deck furniture on the *Titanic*. This message had left John feeling confused and empty. The fear that he had missed God's will for his life lingered. John also shared that recently he had gone to a Christian seminar on moving from success to significance.

At the seminar he had heard joyful testimonies of successful businesspeople who had made a midlife career change. Now they were using their business gifts in Christian organizations and were fully investing their talents for the kingdom. He left the seminar feeling that processing loans simply didn't add up to a significant life. I could not help but empathize with the gnawing ache in John's soul.

A couple of months slipped by, and I caught up with John over another cup of coffee. He had done some studying on his own, probing the rich truths of God's work story found in Scripture. When I asked John what he was learning, he replied, "Tom, I still struggle at times wondering if my work is making much of a difference in the world, but now when I go to work, I don't go with a sense of emptiness lingering in my soul. I go with a sense of expectation that I am honoring God in my work. And my understanding of what it means to take Jesus with me to work has totally changed." As I pressed John a bit further on these changes, he commented, "Being Jesus's apprentice at work has positively changed my attitude, and I am doing more excellent work."

A thick cloud had shrouded John's thinking about discipleship as it related to his faith and work. With these kinds of messages dancing around in John's mind, it's no wonder he felt such a large disconnect between his Sunday church experience and his Monday work experience. This clouded thinking is too often perpetuated by sincere Christian leaders delivering impassioned sermons about the ultimate futility of our work.

Pastoral Malpractice

I, too, have committed what I call pastoral malpractice. Not understanding God's story of work, I spent the majority of my time equipping my congregants for the slimmest segment of their lives. Lamentably, I was much more concerned with how well I did on Sunday than how my congregants did on Monday. My discipleship focus was first on how my congregants could be good Sunday

Christians rather than faithful and fruitful apprentices of Jesus in the places where God had called them to serve him the majority of their week. The painful truth is I am not alone in my pastoral malpractice.

David Miller speaks with compelling clarity about the need for pastoral change: "Whether conscious or unintended, the pulpit all too frequently sends the signal that work in the church matters but work in the world does not. It is perhaps no surprise, then, that workers, businesspeople, and other professionals often feel unsupported by the Sunday church in their Monday marketplace vocations."[8]

For pastors and Christian leaders to communicate, and for us to conclude, that using our gifts in a Christian organization is the only way we can truly invest our talents in the kingdom widely misses the mark of the Bible's theology of vocation. I find John's story all too common among sincere people of faith. Thinking that somehow certain kinds of work are "more Christian" than other kinds; or that only some kinds of work have eternal value, while others do not; or that somewhere in life as we get older we change our work so we can move from success to significance—all of these are unbiblical distortions we must confront in our lives and faith communities.

Our work, no matter how ordinary, can be extraordinary and brimming with God-honoring significance if it is done well for the love of neighbor and for the glory of God. If we are discovering the rich and robust doctrine of vocation for the first time, we might be tempted to see it as merely a passing fad. In our more cynical moments, we might wonder whether all this talk about work is merely the latest hype in an often shallow Christian subculture. Though this kind of thinking about work and its biblical importance may be new to you, the doctrine of Christian vocation is not a fad; it is foundational to an integral Christian faith. A right understanding of vocation has been transforming the day-to-day lives of faithful followers of Jesus for centuries. A proper understanding of vocation requires a robust theology of ordinary, everyday life.

The Goodness of Ordinary Callings

The sixteenth-century Protestant Reformers recognized the urgent need to embrace a biblically centered faith. Over the centuries the gospel of Jesus Christ had become unrecognizable because so much had grown up alongside it. Many things had become more visible than the simple and essential truths of the gospel. The Protestant Reformer Martin Luther pointed the church back to the authority of the Bible and emphasized the priesthood of all believers. This doctrine held that every believer had equal access to God through Jesus Christ and that as each one did their work, be they a farmer or a merchant, they were acting as priests before God.

The Reformation profoundly altered the spiritual formation of many followers of Christ who had languished under the distorted view that the calling to the priesthood, to a monastic community, or to service in the church was a higher, more sacred, more spiritual calling than being a farmer or a merchant. The Reformation reconnected Sunday faith to Monday work.

I always enjoy reading books on history. In his book on the building of the transcontinental railroad, *Nothing like It in the World*, Stephen Ambrose unveils the tremendous courage and challenges that occupied the United States from 1863 to 1869. When we think of this period, we often think about President Lincoln's courageous leadership in freeing a nation from the hideous scourge of slavery. But through Ambrose's book, I learned that another part of Lincoln's lasting legacy was his vision and leadership in building the transcontinental railroad. This massive building project connected our continent and paved the way for an economically developing and politically unified nation.

In a similar way, the sixteenth-century Reformers laid down the theological tracks that reconnected Christian faith with ordinary work. And one of the biblical banners that they heralded was the apostle Paul's inspired words to the church at Corinth: "So, brothers, in whatever condition each was called, there let him remain with

God" (1 Cor. 7:24 ESV). The Reformers rightly pointed out that the apostle Paul promoted the ordinary callings and stations of life, of marriage and singleness, of work and vocation.

The Reformers affirmed that our calling to follow Christ is to be lived out through the conduits of our vocations and stations of life arranged for us under the providence of God. For those who become apprentices of Jesus, their mission in the world is to bloom vocationally where they are providentially planted. It is in our ordinary day-to-day lives of work, rest, and play that we are to flourish, to be salt and light, to be spiritually formed, and to be God's redemptive agents in the world. Our Christian vocation calls each of us to indwell an extraordinary ordinary life. For this is what Jesus himself modeled.

Jesus's life as a carpenter shows us there is no ordinary work. The work God has called you to do is extraordinary. Don't miss out on God's best by taking an ordinary approach to it. Dorothy Sayers was right: "The only Christian work is good work well done."[9] Work with Jesus, work for him, and learn from him how to work. Jesus is not only your Savior and Lord; he is also the greatest workplace mentor you will ever have.

A Prayer of Workplace Apprenticeship

Lord Jesus, in your incarnation you were faithfully present in a Nazareth carpentry shop. You honored the Father not only by your redemptive work on the cross but also by making excellent tables. As your apprentices, may we, too, be faithfully present in our workplaces. Help us to grasp that there is no ordinary work, only extraordinary work done in your name, for the love of our neighbors and for your glory. May the quality of our work honor you and may our work witness to the glory of the gospel and your unimaginable excellence. Amen.

Questions for Reflection and Discussion

- How does Jesus's work as a carpenter change the way you view your work?
- How would your coworkers describe you as a worker?
- What kind of fragrance is wafting through your workplace these days?
- What does the doctrine of the priesthood of all believers say about how you do your work?

Part 2

Your Story

6

Thank God It's Monday

There is wonderful hope beyond the weekend. It involves that very special assignment to which God has called us: our work. And it begins next Monday.

—John Beckett[1]

Now that we have looked through the illuminating window of God's big story of work, we turn our attention to a mirror to help us see how we fit into that story.

I really like dogs, but I have never been much of a cat lover. Yet there is one cat that I have gotten to know pretty well over the years. His name is Garfield, and he holds the Guinness World Record for being the world's most widely syndicated comic strip. There is something about Garfield that resonates with us as people who navigate the challenging contours of our lives and our work. Garfield is often selfish, cynical, sassy, sarcastic, yet surprisingly endearing. Garfield loves watching television, eating food, and getting lots and lots of sleep. Garfield also has a particular fondness for lasagna, something I think he really gets right.

One of the consistent themes of Garfield's lethargic world is how much he hates exercise, diets, and Mondays. Garfield regularly declares, "I am a Friday person in a Monday world." Whether we really like our work or not so much, we can often relate to Garfield's sentiments about Mondays, to imagine them as something we have to push through, to endure, an unavoidable necessity to enjoy the weekends as spaces where we experience the truly good life.

Our culture regularly reinforces living for the weekend, as captured in the acronym TGIF (Thank God it's Friday). We often feel the need for a refuge where we can leave the workweek behind and escape its inevitable hardships and pains. Our weekend focus is most intense in our weekdays. For example, Wednesday is "hump day," after which we're on the downward slope, the weekend inching closer. While weekends and the rest they can bring are good things, living for the weekend will not bring the purpose, fulfillment, and meaning our hearts deeply long for.

As a pastor, I really enjoy visiting with congregants at a local coffee shop. Over sips of coffee and unhurried conversation, I love asking questions of the heart and listening attentively to congregants tell their story. I hear what has shaped them, what they are facing, and the relational, recreational, and vocational dreams they are entertaining. In their words and on their faces, I encounter many disappointments, hurts, fears, and longings. One of the themes I hear most often is the frustration experienced in their work as well as how much they live for the weekends. To them, work is a roadblock to the life they long to live.

It is not bad to look forward to weekends, which often bring rest, recreation, and time to reconnect with family and friends. But living *for* the weekend is another matter. There is much more to life than powering through the week waiting for Friday night to arrive. If you are living too much for the weekends, let me draw your attention to the flashing yellow light on the dashboard of your life. This light may be beckoning your heart to slow down and take careful inventory of your busy and overscheduled life. Do you return to work on

Monday and immediately wish it were the weekend again? In the midst of your work, do you fantasize about the upcoming weekend? Do you count down the days until Friday?

Many factors tempt us to live for the weekend. You may find yourself resenting your tasks and responsibilities. Maybe numbing routines leave you bored and disengaged. The difficult people you have to deal with on the job can wear you out. You may feel perennially exhausted from too much work to do, feeling behind all the time. You may be so tired and depleted that your weekend is mostly a time to catch up on sleep so you can muscle up the energy to tackle the workweek once again. Exhaustion, poor job fit, stress, and workaholism can all leave us living for the weekend. These are real challenges that need our attention. The inconvenient truth is that much of our living for the weekend emerges from an impoverished story of work. You were created for more than the weekends.

The Sunday-to-Monday Gap

An impoverished work story is often the result of what I call a Sunday-to-Monday gap—a disconnect between our Sunday worship and the rest of our work lives. While we may remember the importance of our faith at church on Sunday, it is all too easy to return to our work as if God is absent and our faith is an afterthought. While Sundays are a day to ponder faith, to worship God, Mondays are often framed as "the real world." A dominant cultural narrative increasingly tells us our workplaces are devoid of nonmaterial or transcendent realities.[2] As we work in this disenchanted world, our Sunday faith is tragically left behind on Mondays. All that remains is a shrunken, privatized, leftover faith, making God of little relevance or importance to the workplace.

The great peril of the Sunday-to-Monday gap is that it reduces the "real world" to a materialistic paradigm, shrinking the Christian faith to a quaint portion of our lives, reinforcing a workplace devoid of God's presence, wisdom, and power. Yet the Scriptures tell a different story, one of a God-bathed world, of a triune God who is with us moment by moment, who delights in us, who is always there for us, including in our workplaces. Do you have a Sunday-to-Monday gap in your faith? Do you live your Mondays as if God is continually present or virtually absent? Are you experiencing the "without God" life or the "with God" life at work?

We need another story that challenges the cultural narrative of God's absence and irrelevance in our workplaces and that puts him at the center of our work—a biblical story of work that puts our Monday world in a different perspective, one that transforms us as workers, the work we do, and our workplaces. And we find such a story in the New Testament.

John the Baptist is a fascinating character. In many ways, his unique role in redemptive history is as the opening act for Messiah Jesus. John the Baptist is portrayed by the Gospel writers as a rather eccentric, countercultural guy, yet he plays an important role in paving the way for Messiah Jesus. One of his dominant preaching themes is repentance. "Repentance" is not a word we use every day, but it conveys a watershed moment, a change in our perception and life direction. When John the Baptist calls for repentance, he is communicating the urgent necessity of a turning from and a turning to—a changing of minds and hearts in regard to sin (turning from) and embracing the good news Jesus brings of forgiveness and new creation life (turning to). Repentance aligns our hearts, minds, bodies, and priorities with Jesus's kingdom. For John the Baptist, repentance is multidimensional, and it includes our world of work.

The Gospel of Luke captures John's surprising words as he invites a first-century crowd to align themselves with God's kingdom and Messiah Jesus, who is arriving on the scene. Luke writes, "Tax collectors also came to be baptized, and they asked him, 'Teacher what should we do?' He told them, 'Don't collect any more than what you have been authorized.' Some soldiers also questioned him, 'What should we do?' He said to them, 'Don't take money from anyone by force or false accusation, and be satisfied with your wages'" (3:12–14).

In the first century, both tax collectors and soldiers had bad reputations, for good reason. Both regularly abused the power of their office and extorted the people that Rome ruled over. Tax collectors were required by the Roman government to collect a particular level of taxes, but they collected taxes far beyond that, then pocketed the rest as exorbitant profits and grew wealthy on the backs of the poorest citizens. Soldiers had not only the power of Rome behind them but the power of the sword on them. Soldiers often extorted money from citizens as a kind of quid pro quo protection scheme, not unlike a first-century mafia. Soldiers could ruin someone's life and business on a whim by accusing them of false charges. The falsely accused had little recourse and often faced imprisonment and even death.

John the Baptist speaks into this unjust and hostile environment and calls tax collectors and soldiers to a new work story that challenges the politically sanctioned abuse of power and economic injustice. Importantly, John the Baptist doesn't say, "Stop doing the work of a tax collector or soldier and become a priest." Instead, John the Baptist tells both the tax collector and the soldier to work *differently*. He tells the tax collectors to collect only the tax amount Rome requires. He warns the soldiers not to abuse their power over others or take bribes. Rather than devalue or dismiss their work, John the Baptist *dignifies* it. He tells them their work matters and encourages them to align their work with God's kingdom, ways, and purposes.

When we embrace the good news, we don't leave our work behind for a more "spiritual" calling; rather, our paid and unpaid work takes on a new story—a story of work as God designed it, a story of work as it is, a story of work as it can be, and a story of work as it will be one day in the new heaven and new earth. A story that makes it possible for us to now earnestly say TGIM: "Thank God it's Monday." But if you are going to embrace the good news story in your work world, you will need to begin by reimagining your workplace.

Reimagining Your Workplace

One of the practices I have adopted as a pastor is to visit members of my congregation on the job. For many, it is the first time a pastor has been curious enough to learn about their work. It is also a great joy for me to take on the role of a learner rather than a teacher as well as to pray for them and their work. When I can, I often help them reimagine their work through the clarifying lens of God's story. We talk about God's creation design for work and talk about how echoes of Eden are still present in our paid and unpaid workplaces. We talk about God's continual presence with us, of living and working before an audience of one. We remember together that God is our ultimate boss and will one day give us our most important job review. We recall that our work done unto God and with love for others has lasting significance. As yoked apprentices of Jesus, we talk about how our work aligns with God's kingdom, how the work we do is an embodied, incarnational, and ongoing answer to Jesus's prayer, "Your kingdom come. Your will be done on earth as it is in heaven" (Matt. 6:10). We also remember together how our fellow workers are image bearers of God and how his love is to be directed toward them so that it permeates our workplaces. For Paul's words "Do everything in love" (1 Cor. 16:14) are as important in the workplace as they are in the church.

Wherever God has called you to work, you can enthusiastically say "Thank God it's Monday" if you embrace his story of work. There are three compelling reasons why our workplace really matters: our Monday world is a place we find meaning, a place we worship God, and a place we grow.

A Place We Find Meaning

I had the privilege of spending time with Bob Kern. Mr. Kern, as I addressed him, was a poster child of the greatest generation. Over several decades, with unusual ingenuity, hard work, resilience, and perseverance, Bob built a great company that achieved remarkable growth and financial success. As a man of Christian faith, Bob's work ethic and philanthropic stewardship were unmatched. At lunch one day I asked Mr. Kern what he saw as the greatest need of the emerging generations. Without hesitation, he responded, "So many people today do not know what a meaningful life is or how it is found."[3] Bob Kern knew that a great deal of life's meaning is found in our workplaces. Viktor Frankl knew this too.

In the unspeakable horrors of the Auschwitz concentration camp, Frankl's view of human life was profoundly altered. Trained as a psychiatrist, Frankl brought his own experience to his work. Frankl grasped that while we as humans often seek pleasure and power, our deepest heart longing and greatest daily pursuit is a quest for meaning. Our meaning-seeking is aimed toward our loving relationships, our difficulties and sufferings, and also our places of work: "This uniqueness and singleness which distinguishes each individual and gives meaning to existence has a bearing on creative work as much as it does on human love."[4]

In spite of the inevitable difficulties and trials of every workplace, if you have high regard for your work, if you enjoy, look forward to, and find joy and satisfaction in your work, then you are inhabiting God's story of work. We enter our Monday workplaces hungering for meaning because we were made with this in mind by our Creator God in whom all meaning ultimately originates. We were designed to create and contribute as we embrace the creation mandate, God's job description for us to be fruitful and multiply, to fill the earth and subdue it (Gen. 1:28). Our God is a working God. Made in God's image, we reflect him in our work, working with him and for him in our Monday workplace. This transforming reality brings meaning, assurance, and satisfaction to our daily work.

The Old Testament book of Ecclesiastes addresses our human quest for meaning. The writer paints two contrasting pictures or views of life. On the one hand is the meaninglessness, the inescapable futility we feel if we live, breathe, and work in a godless existence. On the other hand is the energizing meaning we encounter in a God-centered and God-focused life. It is not surprising that Ecclesiastes, a book about meaning, gives so much attention to work.

As the book begins, human work takes center stage with a central question: "What does a person gain for all his efforts that he labors at under the sun?" (Eccles. 1:3). The answer to this question is teased out throughout the book. In essence we discover that without God, work is toilsome and futile, life is empty, and our lives are ultimately meaningless.

Scholar J. Daryl Charles has devoted a great deal of thought to Ecclesiastes and its important message. He writes, "Two outlooks on life and all of reality are on display and being contradistinguished. If life is viewed apart from the Creator, without reference to God and transcendent reality, humans will indeed experience meaninglessness and despair."[5]

Ecclesiastes is sometimes seen as bad news when it comes to the possibility of a meaningful life. It's actually very good news. God designed work in such a way that we can experience meaningful satisfaction in our accomplishments and contribution to others. Do you experience a sense of meaningful contribution and satisfying accomplishment in your workplace? Do you see your work as a gift from God? The writer of Ecclesiastes helps us to see our workplaces as a place of enjoyment: "Here is what I have seen to be good: It is appropriate to eat, drink, and experience good in all the labor one does under the sun during the few days of his life God has given him, because that is his reward. Furthermore, everyone to whom God has given riches and wealth, he has also allowed him to enjoy them, take his reward, and rejoice in his labor. This is a gift of God, for he does not often consider the days of his life because God keeps him occupied with the joy of his heart" (5:18–20).

The workplace God has called you to is a place where meaningful contribution, collaborative relationships, and formidable challenges await.

A Place We Worship God

Where is your primary place of worship? Is it Sunday when you are in church or Monday in your place of work? My wife enjoys serving children in our local church and will often say that children are our greatest teachers. She will often ask the children, "How do we worship God?" They answer, "At church, we pray at meals and bedtime, we read Bible stories." Then she asks, "What will you and your parents be doing tomorrow?" Lots of answers come, but worship is not one of them. She then follows up with, "Did you know that your parent's work can be worship and that your play can be worship?" They respond, "What?!"

This entrenched dichotomy between work and worship speaks volumes. From our earliest development, work and worship are separated in our cognitive frameworks. Work and worship may not be the exact same thing, yet God's story confronts this false dichotomy by painting an integral and seamless reality that our work is to be an essential and central aspect of our God-honoring worship.

While regular weekly worship in a local faith community is vitally important, in fact *all* that we do, wherever we are, is to be an act of worship. Worship is not a one-hour-a-week focus but a whole-life enterprise. While we rightly spend time worshiping God on Sunday, the vast majority of time we spend worshiping God is the rest of the week, while we work. Do you see your workplace as a primary place of worship?

Remembering God Is with You

How do we become more aware of our workplace as a primary place of worship? A helpful way to remember that God is with you at work is to pause before your workday and prayerfully bring to mind that God is always present.[6] Of course, God being with you is true in a broad sense because one of his central attributes is his omnipresence. God is not just always there (wherever *there* is), he is always near to you. Another way to remember God is with you in your workplace is to recognize that your physical body is actually a temple where the Holy Spirit dwells. God's temple is not some building but our living, breathing bodies. As followers of Jesus, whenever we enter our workplaces, we are bringing with us the temple of God.

As the apostle Paul reminds us, "Don't you know that your body is a temple of the Holy Spirit who is in you, whom you have from God? You are not your own, for you were bought at a price. So glorify God with your body" (1 Cor. 6:19–20). The Holy Spirit's indwelling within us has far-reaching implications for our ethical behavior as well as our worship posture. When we embrace this truth, it transforms us as workers and reshapes our workplaces. Our workplace presence means that God is present not only around us but within us. God is with us to shepherd us, to guide us, and to give us wisdom. No matter what our work involves, we are never left to do it alone. A stay-at-home spouse changing diapers and carpooling the kids is not working alone. A teacher grading a student's test is never alone. A businessowner seeking a loan at a bank is never alone. Nor are any of these workers dependent on their own wisdom. A plumber is never alone on the job. God is with them to receive their worshipful work and to provide wisdom, insight, and strength. The Holy Spirit not only indwells us but also desires to empower us for our workplaces.

God's presence means that when we go to work, we are encountering holy ground. How might we begin to reframe our Monday place of worship as holy ground even though it may often feel far from it? Let's remember that when Moses encounters the burning bush, it is in his place of work. What is Moses doing? He is shepherding his father-in-law's sheep. In that workplace encounter, Moses hears God say, "Do not come closer. . . . Remove the sandals from your feet, for the place where you are standing is holy ground" (Exod. 3:5).

Denise Daniels and Shannon Vandewarker describe the daily practice of invoking God's blessing on the holy ground wherever our work is done. They write, "Walking the hallways in prayer, saying a blessing over the office doors in your building, praying for the meeting rooms, the cafeteria, the production spaces within your workplace, the routes where the company cars drive, and asking God's blessing over what happens there—these are all ways of recognizing your workplace as holy ground."[7] In Moses's ordinary workplace, God shows up and is worshiped. You, too, have a burning bush in your workplace, if you are willing to slow down and become more attentive to God's presence there.

When we recognize that our workplace is holy ground, we can better practice the presence of God with us. In my place of work, I have placed visual reminders to help me remember that God is present. As I type these very words on my computer, I remember that I am sitting on holy ground. For you it might be a visual reminder of a Bible verse on your computer screen. Maybe it is something that you put on your daily calendar or a picture on your desk. Perhaps before each daily appointment or meeting, you pause for prayer. Maybe in your daily schedule you build in two or three short breaks in which you remember a verse of Scripture and offer up a prayer of thanksgiving to God. We can sharpen our attentiveness to God's presence by remembering he is with us every time we walk through a door in our workplaces. We all need ways to regularly remember to practice the presence of God throughout the day. Be where your feet are, for that is where God is!

Your workplace is holy ground because God is with you and because the work you do unto him and for the good of others is itself a beautiful act of worship. Your work has not only instrumental value (a means to an end) but intrinsic value—your work *in itself* has value. Most jobs have tasks we don't enjoy but simply need to get done. Dealing with a difficult and demanding customer, addressing conflict with a fellow worker, going into a dirty crawl space to fix a pipe, or cleaning a bathroom may not be enjoyable, but when we embrace this work as an act of God-pleasing worship, the attitude we have and the excellence of our work changes. This, too, is holy work done on holy ground.

A Place We Grow

It is not the typical career path one might expect after receiving a PhD in philosophy from a prestigious university, but Matthew Crawford found himself the owner and operator of Shock Moto, an independent motorcycle repair shop. Working with his hands as a motorcycle mechanic, Matthew Crawford became a strong advocate of manual work, the coherent manner of life it fosters, and its relationship to human flourishing. In his popular book *Shop Class as Soulcraft*, Crawford speaks to the transformational effects our work and our workplaces have in shaping us: "We are accustomed to think of the business world as ruled by an amoral bottom-line mentality, but in fact it is impossible to make sense of the office without noticing that it has become a place of moral education, where souls are formed and a particular ideal of what it means to be a good person is urged upon us."[8] When we think about the Monday world, our tendency is to reflect on how we shape our work, yet we must not overlook how the work we do profoundly shapes us as individuals within a community. The work we do affects the contours of our thinking, develops our competencies, forms many of our relationships, grows our emotional intelligence, and contributes to our manner of feeling and well-being in the world. We shape our work, and our work shapes us.

Growing up in a rural farming community, I grasped early on the powerful effect work had on the people I encountered. I remember as a young boy shaking hands with a neighboring farmer. I politely and respectfully placed my small, smooth hand into his massive hand. With his gentle squeeze, I felt a rush of extraordinary strength. His rough skin and strong calluses spoke volumes to me about the work he did and the person he was. Framing his warm and friendly smile was a tanned, windburned face that reflected many hours toiling beneath the summer sun, caring for farm animals and tilling the rocky earth.

As a young boy, I was enraptured listening to a close-knit group of farmers chatting at the local co-op store. The conversation I heard echoed a particular down-to-earth vocabulary tied to the unpredictable weather patterns, where a timely rain meant the difference between crop success and crop failure. Farmers are people of the land, living with the ebbs and flows of nature and the ever-changing seasons. They are adventurous risk-takers. Seeds are planted with heartfelt hopes, but there is no certainty of a harvest. The work farmers do shapes their competencies; their hearts, minds, and souls; and their broader perspectives about life itself and their particular place in the world. This is true for each one of us, regardless of the work we are called to do.

A professional dancer's body and mind will be formed in a way that is distinct from a surgeon's or a schoolteacher's. The dancer's workplace and the people he works with will speak into his life in enduring ways. Many of his closest friendships will be birthed and sustained in the workplace. A teacher's work is spent exploring the world of ideas. Her competencies are directed toward informing and shaping others' minds. As she influences her students, she, too, is influenced by the very ideas she conveys—often in ways she cannot verbally articulate. On an assembly line a worker will develop a specialized vocabulary, particular relationships, and mental and physical skills that are vastly different from a company CEO, who spends the majority of her time in a corner office or on an airplane going from city to city conducting strategy meetings in preparation for an impending merger.

One car ad describes work's transforming power with these well-chosen words: "The things we make, make us." Theologian Miroslav Volf notes, "Human work is ultimately significant not only because it contributes to the future environment of human beings, but also because it leaves an indelible imprint on their personalities."[9] Our lives and our work are inextricably linked. To a large extent what we do forms much of who we are and who we are becoming.

As a teenager and college student, my work at a Dairy Queen shaped my leadership more than any other work I have been called to. For seven years, Bob, my boss, believed in me, guided my learning, and mentored me in matters of work and life. He saw work as a gift and helped me to see how the Sunday faith we both affirmed found its way into our workplaces. He daily impressed on me the importance of workplace ethics and working diligently. For Bob, the Golden Rule Jesus taught—do to others what you would have them do to you—was the wise and proven path to a healthy workplace culture and a flourishing small business. Bob influenced my life in innumerable ways.

Your work is a gift to you. Like other good gifts of education, marriage, friendship, leisure, and family, your work influences in great measure the person you are becoming. You are daily being formed by the work you do, the people you rub shoulders with, and the skills you acquire. Work is one of the providential arrangements through which you are spiritually formed.

Martin Luther affirmed the central importance of vocation in spiritual formation: "God's complete work is set in motion through vocation."[10] Luther understood that, rather than being an obstacle or impediment to spiritual growth, vocation is the primary pathway God uses to transform our lives. He saw vocation as encompassing a broader theology of the everyday common life, where God-honoring worship and spiritual maturation were the most desired outcomes.

Whether you recognize it or not, your work is shaping you. Is it forming you into a person of increased virtue and greater Christlikeness? Your work is one of God's greatest gifts for your spiritual formation and maturity.

Growing in Christlikeness

Often when we think of spiritual formation, we think of the local church as well as specific practices such as solitude, study, fasting, prayer, and service. This framework is right, good, and important.

For example, a regular discipline of Scripture memory allows us to bring timeless truth to mind throughout the workday. Our engagement in spiritual disciplines is essential for any apprentice of Jesus, but the majority of our life takes place outside of these chosen practices. The ordinary places of life, including our work, not only shape us but can nurture spiritual transformation. The most important place of your spiritual growth is where God has already placed you on Monday. Dallas Willard insightfully speaks to how God's kingdom meets us where God has placed us to serve in our Monday world: "We must accept the circumstances we constantly find ourselves in as the place of God's kingdom and blessing. God has yet to bless anyone except where they actually are, and if we faithlessly discard situation after situation, moment after moment, as not being 'right,' we will simply have no place to receive his kingdom into our life. For those situations and moments are our life."[11] Willard reminds us to be where our feet are, for that is where we are most spiritually formed. This means that your workplace is God's sovereign arrangement for your spiritual growth.

Many times, we see our workplace as an obstacle to spiritual growth rather than an opportunity. You may be thinking, *Tom, you have no idea how godless my workplace is or how corrupt the people I work with are. My workplace feels more like a war zone than holy ground.* I get that. Our workplaces are a space in time where the kingdom of light and the kingdom of darkness often vie for influence. Yet, I can assure you, the nonprofit world in which I work is not sanitized from broken people, difficulties, sin, and spiritual warfare. The apostle Paul reminds us that we can embrace our difficult workplaces with assurance and hope because in the context of suffering, obstacles, and difficulties, we are spiritually formed: "And not only that, but we also boast in our afflictions, because we know that affliction produces endurance, endurance produces proven character, and proven character produces hope. This hope will not disappoint us, because God's love has been poured out in our hearts through the Holy Spirit who was given to us" (Rom. 5:3–5).

Paul faced great difficulties and suffering in his work, and he helps us see that often our hardships are places of our greatest growth. Hardships, difficulties, and suffering often greet us in our workplaces and form our character. They are also profoundly hopeful as we embrace the experiential reality that we are God's beloved, deeply loved and secure in his love. It is often in our broken workplaces where perseverance, proven character, and hope are forged in our lives.

No matter how difficult your work is, with the supernatural resources available to you, you can perform it in the presence and power of the Holy Spirit. A primary place we learn to walk in the Spirit is in our Monday workplace. Paul beautifully describes these character qualities of those who walk and work in the Spirit: "The fruit of the Spirit is love, joy, peace, patience, kindness, goodness, faithfulness, gentleness, and self-control" (Gal. 5:22–23). If your coworkers were to describe you, would they include these qualities? No matter whether your work is paid or unpaid, and regardless what sector you serve in, God has providentially placed you there and empowers you to live a Spirit-filled life.

I was delighted to receive an email from a stay-at-home mom who is bringing God's story into her daily work. She writes, "A stay at home mom doesn't get a lot of accolades or affirmation. No paycheck. No glowing review from their boss. I have been working through these thoughts and feelings and several weeks ago decided I wasn't going to spend any more time feeling like a victim. I have had a new outlook on life over these past few weeks and I feel so much better. I have never thought of being a mother as an act of worship. I can look at it in a whole new way now. I can now see the contributions I make to my household as what I was uniquely created to do for this season of life."

Is there a Sunday-to-Monday gap in your thinking? Are you compartmentalizing your work and worship or are you seeing your daily work through an integral and seamless lens? God deeply desires that in your workplace you will experience life-giving meaning, joyful worship, and transformational spiritual growth. Your work is not an obstacle to your spiritual growth but rather a providential conduit for it. God, in his unfathomable love and grace, has invested much in you and your spiritual growth. Will you reframe your Monday workplace with God's story? If you will, you can enthusiastically say, "Thank God it's Monday."

A Prayer for Monday

Heavenly Father, thank you for making me for more than the weekend. Lord Jesus, help me to see my workplace as a worship space in which to enjoy and know you, a place of spiritual formation. Holy Spirit, thank you that I never work alone. Fill me. Shape me. Walk with me. Today. Amen.

Questions for Reflection and Discussion

- Whatever you may be experiencing, if Jesus were in your shoes right now, how would he handle this?
- How might you see your workplace as a place of spiritual formation?
- What simple practice can you adopt to claim God is with you and for you in your workplace?
- What simple practice can help remind you that your workplace is holy ground?
- Who encouraged or mentored you in a way that has shaped who you have become today? Was it someone in your workplace?

7

Neighborly Love

God does not need our good works, but our neighbor does.

—Martin Luther[1]

Not many days go by when I do not find myself in a coffee shop. I love coffee's rich aroma and bold flavor and the sensation of a piping-hot mug on a cold morning. I also feel a sense of gratitude for the kind and helpful barista who greets me, takes my order, and presents to me a well-crafted morning brewed masterpiece. As a matter of habit and courtesy, I usually say thank you, but often I fail to reflect on the many hands it took to get my day off to a great start. I completely forget all the effort and hard work that was poured into my mug of coffee on those crisp mornings.

Think with me for a moment about the coffee farmers and the many hands who grew and picked the coffee beans, the many workers who processed, packaged, and transported the coffee beans from someplace around the globe to my local coffee shop. My delicious cup of coffee also needed skilled hands to roast it and brew it, and it required manufactured equipment precisely designed to bring it to the right temperature. Utility companies provided reliable electricity and clean supplies of water. A whole host of hands designed, manufactured, and transported the brewing equipment, along with the paper cups and many serving accessories vital to a coffee shop's operation. From the initial planting of coffee beans to the final pour, a myriad of financial entities and transactions took place on computer screens guided by a free-market price allocation based on ever-changing supply and demand realities. Many minds, feet, and hands make possible one mug of coffee.

The term we use to describe the interactive, interdependent, collaborative effort necessary to provide goods and services is a supply chain. When this complex interdependence is disrupted, our modern economy grinds to a halt, and our daily lives are impacted. The cup of coffee I anticipate on my morning drive simply will not be there when I want it. The supply chain we rely on for just about everything we need is really a supply chain of neighborly love. Whether every worker in that complex supply chain realizes it or not, they love others in and through their work. These workers may think the work they do is only a means to a paycheck, yet through their work, they embody love for me as one of their neighbors, a neighbor most of them will not know or ever meet.

When we reflect on the paid and unpaid work we do, we begin to recognize that it matters to others more than we may realize. Our Monday work is a vital part of a supply chain, or what we might call a neighborly love chain. Our workplaces are not just places where we worship God, find meaning, and grow spiritually. They are also a primary place we are called to love others in an interdependent global economy.

A Primary Place to Love Others

We often think of our work through an individualist lens. We view it as an instrumental means for our personal accomplishment, a sense of satisfaction, and a way to pay the bills and provide financial security. This individualist lens is not necessarily a bad thing, nor does it equate to a self-absorbed blindness, but it often proves to be impoverished. What if we looked at the paid and unpaid work we are called to do through the lens of loving others? What if we understood our work to be a God-designed opportunity for loving our neighbors near and far? What if our workplaces are the very places God calls us to be his loving ambassador, reflecting his love for other cherished image bearers?

The illuminating and transformational lens of one of Jesus's most foundational teachings helps us to see our workplaces differently. This theological microburst is called the Great Commandment.

The Great Commandment

Jesus taught that loving God and our neighbor is at the very heart of Christian faith. But what does loving our neighbor look like in our Monday worlds? For many followers of Jesus, neighborly love is taking soup to someone when they are sick or mowing a friend's lawn when they are on vacation. These tangible, voluntary gestures of love are good and right, but what if when Jesus spoke about neighborly love, he also had our work in mind? What if the *primary* way we love our neighbors is through our work? What if neighborly love fuels the economic flourishing of our neighbor in an increasingly globally interconnected world?

Jesus talked more about work, money, and economics than we might imagine. Most of Jesus's parables reflect the agrarian economy of the first century. As Klaus Issler notes, "Of the thirty-seven parables in the Synoptic Gospels (Matthew, Mark, and Luke), thirty-two mention some form of work-related activity as part of the storyline."[2] Understanding Jesus's work, economic knowledge, and competency should not be surprising when we realize he spent the majority of his life learning a carpentry trade and running a small business. In Jesus's first-century context, he was known first and foremost as a carpenter from Nazareth (Mark 6:1–3).

When Jesus became an itinerant rabbi, his preaching often took place in a marketplace surrounded by buyers and sellers. We must not miss that Jesus looked to work as a primary place we embody love for God and others. Taking a closer look at chapter 10 of Luke's Gospel, we discover transforming insight framed around a revealing conversation Jesus had and a riveting story he tells.

In chapter 10, Luke gives us a front-row seat to a conversation Jesus has with a lawyer who's an expert on the Old Testament. The expert asks Jesus how one inherits eternal life, and Jesus responds with a follow-up question: What does the Old Testament say about that? The man wisely responds with what has come to be known as the Great Commandment: "You shall love the Lord God with all your heart and with all your soul and with all your strength and with all your mind, and your neighbor as yourself" (Luke 10:27 ESV).[3] After affirming the lawyer's wise insight extracted from two Old Testament texts,[4] Jesus simply tells him to embody this truth, to live it out every day. It may seem Jesus's assertion would end the conversation, but more awaits us.

Luke provides a glimpse into the lawyer's motivation: he is more interested in discrediting Jesus than in learning from him. The heart of the lawyer's problem was his self-righteousness, seeking to be accepted before God on his own merit. The door of this lawyer's heart was cracked open enough for all to see the gap between what he knew was true and right and how he actually lived. Exposed and evasive, prideful and perturbed, the lawyer retorts, "Who is my neighbor?" Rather than giving him a pat answer, Jesus tells an unforgettable story. It not only addresses the question but also gives insight into another very important question: *What does loving my neighbor really mean?*

Jesus tells a story of a man who was making the arduous seventeen-mile trek from Jerusalem to Jericho. Along the way, this man, likely a Jew, becomes a victim of thugs who rob him, beat him, and leave him for dead. Meanwhile, a Jewish priest who is making his way on the same road comes by, but he keeps walking. Although we are curious, Jesus doesn't tell us what this religious leader is thinking. Perhaps in his heart and mind an intense tug-of-war ensues. Should he maintain ritual purity or seek to aid a needy stranger who may already be dead? The ethical tug-of-war doesn't last long. The priest keeps his pace, leaving a desperate stranger lying by the road woefully vulnerable and unattended. But not all hope is lost.

A glimmer of promise enters the storyline as another religious leader, a Jewish Levite, is traveling on the same road. For whatever reason, just like the priest, the Levite also walks right by the man. Things are looking increasingly grim until a Samaritan comes walking by. It is likely that the Samaritan was not a religious leader but rather a person of commerce seeking to engage in a business transaction in Jericho. Strategically located on routes of trade, Jericho was a center of economic activity in the first century.

Both racially and religiously, Jews looked down on Samaritans. Yet in Jesus's story, the Samaritan crosses formidable barriers of human indifference, racial bigotry, and religious prejudice to offer aid for the Jewish man left for dead. The Samaritan does even more, halting his business trip to take a Jewish neighbor to an inn for healing and recovery.

The surprising hero of Jesus's story is not a Jewish religious leader but a despised and often ostracized Samaritan. The priest, Levite, and Samaritan all saw the man who had been robbed, beaten, and left for dead. But only the Samaritan saw him through the compassionate lens of neighborly love. What a riveting contrast Jesus presents in the story. The bigotry and hypocrisy of the Jewish Levite and priest is contrasted with the true compassion of the Samaritan businessperson.

In telling this story, Jesus employs an important word that expresses intense feelings of empathy, feelings that are so intense, they often produce physiological effects, such as groans, tears, or pangs. Jesus also uses the word "empathy" in the parable of the prodigal son (Luke 15:11–32). The English translation is "compassion."[5] Elsewhere, Jesus makes the point in the parable of the prodigal son that when the father sees the son making his way back home, he has "compassion" on him. After going to a far country and squandering the family inheritance and ending up destitute, the father still sees him as his son, feels empathy for him, and expresses generous love to him.

With his specific word choice, Luke is saying in the parable of the neighborly Samaritan that unlike the two religious leaders, the Samaritan businessman saw the man left for dead by the road not as a Jew or a Samaritan but as his own needy son. Woven into this beautiful tapestry of compassion is a familial love overflowing with empathy and action for a stranger who is treated like a member of the family. Through his story, Jesus teaches that neighborly love is merely an extension of family love. A neighbor properly understood is a fellow image bearer of God, a member of the family of humanity.

Jesus's surprising story showcases the amazing generosity of the Samaritan, who does more than offer first aid. Like the generous father in the parable of the prodigal son, who puts a ring on his son's finger and shoes on his feet, the Samaritan businessman pulls out his credit card and guarantees payment for whatever the robbed and injured man will need to recover from this crisis.

In Jesus's story, we observe a riveting contrast between the callous indifference of the religious leaders and the heartfelt compassion of a Samaritan businessperson. But Jesus makes a more subtle contrast in the story between the economic injustice of the robbers and the economic capacity and generosity of the Samaritan businessman. Jesus draws a distinction between the robbers wrongly taking what is not theirs and the Samaritan generously giving what is rightfully his. As biblical scholar Kenneth Bailey notes, the parable is literarily arranged with seven scenes, bookended by an economic contrast: "In scene 1 the robbers take all the man's possessions, and in scene 7 the Samaritan pays for the man out of his own resources because the man has nothing."[6] Jesus wants his hearers to understand that loving neighbors in need involves both compassion and economic capacity. Jesus goes out of his way to describe not only the loving compassion of the Samaritan but also the embodiment of that love in and through the economic generosity he exhibited. Properly understood, neighborly love calls for truth, grace, and mercy to put on economic hands and feet.

The Hands of Neighborly Love

What made it possible for the Samaritan businessperson to help his needy neighbor get back on his feet? Certainly, the Samaritan was motivated by heartfelt compassion, but he was only able to engage in loving action because his occupation had given him capacity to do so. The Samaritan's embodiment of love with its economic capacity came from the diligent labor and wise financial stewardship he embraced within an economic system of adding value to others.

If we are to love our neighbors in accordance with Jesus's teaching, both heartfelt compassion and economic capacity are needed. Economists Victor Claar and Robin Klay help us see that our work "supplies the physical, psychological, artistic, and religious needs of communities extending to the ends of the earth. Furthermore, through work, we create abundance out of which we help meet the needs of others."[7] If we are going to love our neighbor well, it is often made possible because we have the capacity to do so in and through our work. Distinguished economist Thomas Sowell emphasizes the need for economic capacity in caring for our under-resourced neighbors: "Ultimately, it is economic prosperity which makes it possible for billions of dollars to be devoted to helping the less fortunate."[8]

The gospel compels us to show neighborly love that is tangible and economically embodied. The apostle John puts it this way: "If anyone has this world's goods and sees a fellow believer in need but withholds compassion from him—how does God's love reside in him? Little children, let us not love in word or speech, but in action and in truth" (1 John 3:17–18). The apostle Paul teaches that the gospel transforms not only our work but also our economic life. He states, "Let the thief no longer steal, but rather let him labor, doing honest work with his own hands, so that he may have something to share with anyone in need" (Eph. 4:28 ESV). Do we grasp what Paul is saying? The gospel not only addresses our greatest impoverishment, which is spiritual impoverishment, but also presses into other everyday realities and compels us to address economic impoverishment. The gospel compels us to live in such a God-honoring way that we do good and honest work that adds value to our neighbor. In this good work, we can make an honest profit and cultivate economic capacity so that we can serve others and help meet their needs. Our diligent work creates economic value, which makes it possible for us to live generously and for neighborly love.

The Best Workers Make the Best Neighbors

Martin Luther said it well: "God does not need our good works, but our neighbor does."[9] A primary way God designed us to love our neighbors is by working well, which helps us generate a capacity to serve others and be generous to them in their time of need. When it comes to being a helpful neighbor, a slothful worker faces a steep uphill climb. The best workers make the best neighbors.

Apprentices of Jesus are called to be generous with their time, talents, acts of kindness, and faithful prayers for others. We are commissioned to be generous in sharing the gospel with our neighbors, but we are also called to be generous with the resources that come from our diligent labor and wise financial management. How can we be generous in tangibly caring for our neighbor if we have nothing left to give?

Dallas Willard adds insight about the posture of neighborly love in the workplace: "The task of Christian spokespersons, leaders, and professionals is to exemplify and teach foundational traits of the good life Jesus manifests. But this must also include the more specific traits required in the public domain—industriousness, self-control, moderation and responsibility for oneself and others. That is the responsibility and posture of love. The human drive to be self-supporting can be tied to a determination to be productive in order to bless others."[10]

The Great Commandment challenges us to bring God's story of work into our Monday worlds by nurturing compassionate hearts and by embodying Great Commandment love in and through our work-related economic capacity. Economic capacity does not appear out of thin air. It comes from our hard work, value creation, and faithful vocational stewardship. Neighborly love requires both compassion and capacity.

How much good could the Samaritan have done if he hadn't worked hard as a businessman? When we think about helping our neighbor, we ought to think first about our work and the value it creates for others in a modern economy. We also should consider how the resources our work produces allow us to provide for our families and ourselves as well as to further the common good.

At times I struggle to keep a good attitude when I pay my taxes. My tax bill always seems way too high, and I don't always appreciate how governments make tax policy and spend citizens' money. Yet I realize the Bible encourages me to be a good earthly citizen by paying my taxes, and when I view my payment through the lens of neighborly love, it alters my attitude. The wealth we accumulate through the work we do provides for protections and services that my fellow citizens and I benefit from via taxes. Taxes on my compensated work and wealth make a functioning government and various civic goods possible. The income I receive from my work also allows me to tithe to my church and give to nonprofits, furthering the common good and the kingdom of God.

The Bible speaks a great deal about our responsibility to care for others, particularly the poor and vulnerable, but how do we do that? Economists Brian Fikkert and Steve Corbett help us to comprehend the complexities of human impoverishment and reminds us that, in spite of our best intentions and philanthropic efforts, we can actually hurt the poor instead of helping them. Fikkert and Corbett write, "'Spending yourself' often involves more than giving a handout to a poor person, a handout may very well do more harm than good."[11] Both the generation of wealth and the stewardship of economic capacity through diligent work need biblical love and wisdom to guide it. You won't be able to love your neighbor well if you don't understand economics well. Human flourishing and economic flourishing go hand in hand, and our daily work plays an essential role.[12]

When Neighborly Love Is Absent

I experienced the absence of neighborly love as a young boy who grew up in rural poverty. My father's untimely death amplified the number of times my six siblings and I faced material impoverishment. During our daily bus rides home from school, our poverty could not be masked or hidden. On more than one occasion, one of us was asked, "When are you going to paint your house?" We tried to hide our need, offering up some plausible yet deceptive reason for the glaringly neglected appearance of our house.

Even as a ten-year-old boy, I knew house paint was a luxury far beyond our single mother's meager budget. Although I had little economic understanding at the time, I knew the world I'd been born into was an economic one and that the economics of a family mattered. And though she never spoke a single complaining word, I also knew it was a herculean struggle for my mom to make sure we had enough food on the table. The exterior of the house would have to wait, and wait, and wait. The intrusive questions and puzzled looks; the disapproving stares and the snide snickers; the shame, the fears, and the feeling of inferiority that material impoverishment brought to us continued and continued. The bus ride home from school was a regular and unwelcome reminder that we were poor. And that reminder often prompted me to question my own worth and value.

One of the most painful and lingering memories from my early adolescence occurred after a softball game with a few friends. I found myself at a drive-in restaurant where I realized I could not afford a single item on the menu. Suddenly I wasn't hungry anymore. As a young boy, I courageously fought back the tears while I stood beside my friends. But when I got home that night, I drenched my pillow in a flood of sorrow. Though I had not yet taken an economics class or heard the names of Friedman, Hayek, and Keynes, I knew in the depths of my heart that economics mattered—a lot. I couldn't articulate it at the moment, but I began to grasp on a very personal level that economic flourishing and human flourishing were intricately connected. In spite of her hard work, my single mom faced overwhelming challenges. How she needed neighborly love to be extended to her. A neighborly love not merely of compassion but also of capacity and the wise stewardship of others' wise philanthropy. My mom needed generous Samaritans around her, but tragically there were few, if any.

While the Samaritan in Jesus's story incarnated neighborly love, so did the innkeeper whose business provided an important service for the traveler. Unlike the perpetrators of injustice who robbed the Jewish man and left him for dead by the road, the innkeeper maintained a helpful business to serve others' needs. An important aspect of being an image bearer of God is to create value in serving others. While some economic systems contribute to human flourishing better than others, there is no perfect economic system. Affirming a free-market approach, theologian Wayne Grudem and economist Barry Asmus offer a helpful perspective: "Compared to perfection, the free market is easy to criticize. Utopia is always a better idea. But compared to any real world example ever tried in the past, its virtues of greater economic productivity, of lifting the masses from poverty, of promoting virtuous behavior, and of frequent personal benevolence are unsurpassed."[13]

Although there is much to commend about a free-market economy, not all workers worldwide are paid a fair wage or treated well; some of this is essentially exploitative slave labor. Also, significant economic and wealth disparities are things that continually need to be addressed.

Followers of Christ work in broken workplaces within broken economic systems. Yet we are called to be agents of redemption, incarnating neighborly love in our Monday world. Work was never designed to be merely a solitary enterprise; it is woven into the fabric of flourishing human community. Doing our work well matters to God and to our neighbor. The best workers make for the best neighbors.

Christian Love in the Workplace

We express our neighborly love not only in and through the work we are called to do but also in the way we work. Neighborly love is more about how we work than where we work and who lives near us. As followers of Jesus, we bring the fruit of the Spirit into our work and workplace culture. The character qualities we exhibit are the basic ingredients for a flourishing workplace culture. Preeminent among them is the Christian love that the apostle Paul describes: "Love is patient, love is kind. Love does not envy, is not boastful, is not arrogant, is not rude, is not self-seeking, is not irritable, and does not keep a record of wrongs. Love finds no joy in unrighteousness but rejoices in the truth. It bears all things, believes all things, hopes all things, endures all things. Love never ends" (1 Cor. 13:4–8). Apply Paul's beautiful description of Christian love to the context of your daily work. How would your workplace culture change if love were modeled by fellow employees in their interactions? What about the many customers or stakeholders of the organization you serve? Imagine the increased trust, harmony, productivity, innovation, creativity, and satisfaction. How differently would you approach your work if modeling the fruit of the Spirit and the virtue of love became your prayerful consideration and highest aim? If you asked the apostle Paul to name the most important thing to remember as you enter your workweek, I believe that in addition to doing your job well, he would say love others well. Encouraging the first-century followers of Jesus in Corinth, Paul writes, "Do everything in love" (1 Cor. 16:14). Paul's timeless words would transform our work and workplaces if they were heeded and embodied in the power of the Holy Spirit. Perhaps what our workplaces need most is neighborly love.

I received an email from a follower of Jesus whose US-based technology company does a good deal of international business and employs a talented workforce in India. Tim is a modern-day Samaritan businessperson doing good work, seeking to embody neighborly love in his Monday world and loving his neighbors in India. Tim's employees experience meaningful work, deepen relationships with fellow workers, and achieve financial stability and growth. Tim writes, "What I have come to realize is that my position of influence puts me in a unique position as a Christian. My workers in India are decent, hardworking, college educated, and have a desire to live a good life. I pay a fair wage and offer a path to economic freedom. During my many visits to India, they've told me that my values seem different from many perceptions they have of Americans. . . . I've been able to share my faith and values with a group that is willing to listen. My neighbors in India now have a larger stake in a stable world since they are connected to the world economy. Their prosperity trickles down into their community. And hopefully they see a little of the love of Jesus reflected through me."[14]

The posture of Christian love, of the neighborly love we are to adopt and embody in our workplaces, is one that cares for and advocates for others, addresses injustices, seeks fairness for all stakeholders, and provides opportunities, especially for the disadvantaged and under-resourced. When your colleagues or customers describe what it is like working with you, what do they say? Do their words echo the fruit of the Spirit, the virtue of Christian love? Does your virtue and love point them to the goodness of God and the brilliance, beauty, and sacrificial love of Jesus? We may not be in a position of great influence in our workplace, but we can create what organizational expert Jim Collins has called pockets of greatness.[15] We can bring pockets of Christlike neighborly love into our Monday world.

A Sacrificial Love

The Samaritan businessman not only loved his neighbor with abundant financial generosity but also risked his life for his neighbor. With all the hatred, bigotry, and prejudice Jews had toward Samaritans at that time in history, the Samaritan faced the real possibility of threat and hostility upon arriving at the inn.

While the risky compassion and generous capacity of the Samaritan is stunning, we dare not overlook that Jesus ultimately points to himself in telling this story. Jesus not only risks his life but also lays it down on the cross for us. No matter our physical health or economic condition, we are that person beaten and left for dead. We need Christ's compassion and sacrifice as we are helpless and utterly without hope. Jesus the ultimate good neighbor had both the compassion and capacity to rescue us. Jesus is our neighbor who took on human flesh and lived among us (John 1:14). He demonstrated in his faithful work in the carpentry shop and in his atoning work on the cross the highest expression of neighborly love. The world needs your work of neighborly love that is embodied and tangibly manifested by a fruitful and productive life in your Monday workplace.

A Prayer of Neighborly Love

Heavenly Father, thank you for your great love for us. It is in our love for you that we ask for help in building our compassion and capacity to creatively seek the good of those you have placed in our lives. Help me to remember that my daily work is primarily how I love my neighbor. In Jesus's name, Amen.

Questions for Reflection and Discussion

- How does your understanding of work change when seen through the lens of a supply chain of neighborly love?

- Why is it important to grasp that loving your neighbor involves both Christian compassion to empathize as well as economic capacity to meet needs?

- What does virtuous love look like when it is embodied with colleagues, customers, and stakeholders?

- How might you nurture greater neighborly love in your workplace culture?

- How does Jesus not only model neighborly love but also become for you the ultimate good neighbor?

8

Avoiding Burnout

Not many of us claim to be God, but our unrealistic expectations for our work, our children, our bodies, our churches—for just about every aspect of our lives—show that we actually do imagine that we are God. We act as if we should never grow tired or weary, that we could and should always do more and be more.

—Kelly Kapic[1]

John Lennon and Paul McCartney wrote a song that captured the angst of a generation. A song with just one word for its title: "Help!" Though it was written many years ago, it captures the heart cry I hear in so many of my conversations. It is a cry for help in the depressing, debilitating black hole of burnout. In decades of organizational leadership and pastoral experience, I have not seen this level of emotional, spiritual, relational, and physical depletion.

"I Don't Think I Can Do This Anymore"

A Mayo Clinic–trained pathologist who has a distinguished career in Kansas City texted me recently that he was on the edge of burnout. We met at a local coffee shop, where he described to me the overwhelming work he is navigating, including staffing shortages, longer hours, exhaustion, and a host of technological changes and economic pressures. The quiet desperation on his face was articulated as he said, "I don't think I can do this anymore."

Perhaps that is where you find yourself in your work world, or maybe you feel like you are moving quickly in that dire direction. Maybe a colleague or close friend is in the black hole of burnout and you are not sure how to help.

In a report on burnout in the medical profession, the *Wall Street Journal* recently noted that "hospitals have been chronically understaffed and nurses and doctors complain of high stress and exhaustion. In a survey of more than 12,500 nurses by the research affiliate of the American Nurses Association, 43 percent of nurses said they were burned out."[2]

But burnout is rampant everywhere, not just in the medical profession. I have many conversations with those in people-intensive vocations whose health and well-being are deteriorating. Their words to me are almost verbatim "I don't think I can do this anymore."[3] Why does burnout seem to be on the rise everywhere we look? Why do so many of us feel like we are running on empty? Intensifying cultural change and pressure is one contributing factor.

Increasing cultural macro-pressures are fueling burnout. We sense in unsettling and disorienting ways what the psalmist declared long ago: "When the foundations are destroyed, what can the righteous do?" (Ps. 11:3). The very worldview and ethical foundations we have stood on are crumbling around us. The way many people have come to understand faith itself, our sense of self-identity, and our formation as apprentices of Jesus in an increasingly secular framework has profoundly changed.[4] In 2023, the nonprofit Renovaré convened eleven roundtables with thirty-five leaders from a wide array of sectors including arts, media, technology, politics, mental health, higher education, Christian nonprofits, and the church. From that group of thought leaders, four macro-themes emerged around our cultural moment and context. First, we live in a time of deep instability manifesting in panic, isolation, and loneliness. Second, there is a great deal of polarization and breakdown across institutions, including the church. Third, more and more people don't know who they are, whose they are, what is true, or where they belong. Fourth, there is growing evidence of the widescale loss of confidence in leaders because of abuses of power and tragic character flaws.[5]

The increased overload in the workplace, the overwhelming bombardment of information, and the dizzying amount of technological change are all contributing to the emotional, spiritual, relational, and physical depletion of burnout. And if our job description depletes us of energy rather than giving us energy to do what we love, we are much more susceptible to burnout.[6] At burnout level, stress doesn't care about our deadlines. High levels of stress create a ticking time bomb ready to explode.

A Burned-Out Prophet

While the term "burnout" is relatively new, the Old Testament records the story of someone who had a big burnout moment. His name was Elijah, and he worked as a prophet. Prophets served as spokespersons for God to communicate divine words to his covenant people and speak truth to power. We find Elijah's story in the book of 1 Kings. Elijah has expended great energy in his work, confronting the false gods of Baal and achieving a visible milestone of victory. Yet immediately following this workplace success, Elijah goes into emotional free fall. The powerful and ruthless queen Jezebel sends a message to Elijah that he is a dead man walking. With a contract out on his head, Elijah breaks down in fear and runs for his life to a far barren wilderness. Running on empty and frozen in fear, Elijah hits rock bottom and cries out to God: "But he went on a day's journey into the wilderness. He sat down under a broom tree and prayed that he might die. He said, 'I have had enough! LORD, take my life, for I'm no better than my ancestors'" (1 Kings 19:4).

After expending so much spiritual, emotional, and physical energy, Elijah is all out of gas. This level of exhaustion and depletion not only numbs courage, it evaporates hope. In this black hole of burnout, Elijah feels exhausted and desperately alone. At that point, death seems the best way out of his misery and overwhelming hopelessness.

The rest of Elijah's story reveals that through both supernatural and natural interventions, he bounces back from burnout to resilience. Elijah needs bodily replenishment through some badly overdue sleep as well as nourishing food. God sees to it that Elijah gets a nap and a snack. In addition, God lets Elijah know he is not alone and gives him a forty-day break from his work for rest, restoration, and replenishment.[7] When we are burned out it takes longer to recover because a day or two's rest doesn't relieve the exhaustion and hopelessness. Elijah's story is both sobering as well as hopeful for us. Workplace burnout does not have to stop us in our tracks, define us, or prevent a good future. Few of us are called to be a prophet confronting idolatry and speaking truth to power. However, if we are going to reverse the tide on workplace burnout, self-care in and out of the workplace will be crucial.

On the Precipice of Burnout

Over the course of several decades, I have had the privilege of serving in nonprofit leadership. Whether facing the demands of entrepreneurship or moving an organization to greater health and missional effectiveness, I have at times found myself on the precipice of burnout. Burnout is a very overwhelming, lonely, and hopeless place. Yet as I approached the valley of the shadow of burnout, I discovered some impoverished theology that needed attention and correction. I had viewed the idea of self-care as inherently selfish rather than a high stewardship both as a follower of Jesus and as a servant leader. I knew that the Great Commandment to love God was of high importance, but what I did not grasp as fully was loving my neighbor "as myself."

Embedded in Jesus's teaching on the Great Commandment is the proper ordering of our loves, including a proper love of ourselves as an image bearer and beloved child of God. Self-care properly understood involves attending to ourselves so that out of the overflow of well-being we can be fully present and faithful in what God has called us to be and do. We cannot give what we don't have, and we cannot lead well unless it is out of an overflow of our own flourishing minds, hearts, bodies, and souls. A regular assessment of our own well-being is paramount in stewarding the life God has so graciously given us.

Burnout or Resilience?

The main difference between a life of resilient flourishing and one of burnout is the ongoing attentiveness to one's self-care, a recognition that holistic well-being is a daily pursuit. The most important aspect of self-care is a flourishing spiritual formation centered in apprenticeship with Jesus. A foundational element of burnout is a lack of ongoing spiritual formation and vitality, of daily experiencing the empowering and life-giving presence of Christ. Jesus himself guides us into the path of human flourishing. He is the lamp to our feet and the light to our path. In Matthew's Gospel, Jesus extends to us the great invitation to human flourishing. Jesus says, "Come to Me, all who are weary and heavy-laden, and I will give you rest. Take My yoke upon you and learn from Me, for I am gentle and humble in heart, and you will find rest for your souls. For My yoke is easy and My burden is light" (Matt. 11:28–30 NASB 1995).

Jesus invites us to an intimate apprenticeship. In this text, notice that Jesus repeats "rest" twice. By using the word "rest," Jesus is looking back at God's perfect design for human flourishing recorded for us in Genesis 1, where after six days, God rested. Rest here encapsulates the flourishing life God desires and intends for us to experience in and through Jesus as we put on his yoke. It is being yoked with Jesus in the power of the Spirit in a local church community where we experience the deepening intimacy of the "with God" life. Jesus invites us to a life of rest, where we know and are intimately known by Christ.

In The Message paraphrase, Eugene Peterson captures Jesus's invitation beautifully: "Are you tired? Worn out? Burned out on religion? Come to me. Get away with me and you'll recover your life. I'll show you how to take a real rest. Walk with me and work with me—watch how I do it. Learn the unforced rhythms of grace. I won't lay anything heavy or ill-fitting on you. Keep company with me and you'll learn to live freely and lightly" (Matt. 11:23–30 MSG). When we put on Jesus's yoke, we embrace his precepts and practices. We obey what he taught and live how he lived. Walking in step with him, we increasingly learn how to live as if he were us. In his training yoke, we learn the rhythms of the flourishing life, what Peterson describes as the "unforced rhythms of grace." As we learn from the Good Shepherd in the midst of the noisy clamor of our lives and our world, we lie down in green pastures, we are led beside still waters, and our souls are replenished and restored.

One of the great privileges of my life was to spend time with Dallas Willard, one of the most brilliant and Christlike persons I have ever known. He was once asked what one word he thought best described Jesus. Dallas paused for a moment and then responded, "relaxed."[8]

How would you answer that question? What word comes first to your mind? From the New Testament accounts of Jesus's life and work we can see that he modeled a life of sacrifice, but he also modeled a flourishing life, one that embraced self-care at a sustainable pace, healthy patterns, and life-giving people. There is no indication that Jesus ever faced burnout. It is a good reminder for us that

Jesus did not try to meet every human need or request. He said no. Like us, Jesus experienced human limitations. If Jesus said no to people and to more work, so can we. He regularly pursued his own self-care and spiritual disciplines, nurturing intimacy with the Father.[9] In the midst of such an overwhelming mountain of human need, Jesus encouraged his disciples to embrace self-care. His wise and tender words to them are also directed to us: "Come away by yourselves to a remote place and rest for a while" (Mark 6:31).[10] As we consider a path forward from perilous exhaustion and burnout to one of joyful flourishing and buoyant resilience, we must give attention to our pace, our patterns, and our people.

How Is Your Pace?

We live in an age of busyness, driven by our spiritual and relational impoverishment and 24-7 technology. In our modern world, the once-flourishing rhythm of day and night is now blurred. Remote work also blurs the boundaries we once had between home and office. How do those of us who work at home step away from our paid work?

A healthy sustainable pace might look different for each one of us depending on our differing mental, physical, and emotional capacities, and we all have limits. I find I have a propensity to embrace too fast a pace, to work too many hours. I was talking with a colleague about how we could nourish well-being with our senior leaders. He commented that due to the emotional energy expended in the people-intensive work we do, we not only need to monitor the number of hours we and our teams work but must also pay attention to the weighty nature of those hours. In seeking a sustainable pace, it is important to acknowledge that not all hours of work are the same in what they extract from us, the toll they have on our minds, hearts, souls, and bodies. We often need to slow down in terms of not just our physical energy but also our emotional energy. In many cases the higher level of leadership and responsibility we have in a business or organization, the more time we need for rest, reflection, and creative thought. Burnout is not merely physical exhaustion from working too many hours; it is also emotional exhaustion that inevitably comes from the weight of those hours.

Eliminating Hurry

Embracing a sustainable pace will mean for most of us slowing down and saying no more often. Few things are more perilous to one's well-being, relationships, and vocational effectiveness than a fast-paced lifestyle manifested in overpacked daily and weekly schedules. Dallas Willard wisely told a pastor that the most important change he could make in his life was to "ruthlessly eliminate hurry from your life." When this pastor asked Dallas what else he should do, Dallas told him that if he got a handle on eliminating hurry, the rest of his life and work would be set on a path of flourishing rather than burnout.[11]

A hurried, distracted, shallow, inattentive life is the default lifestyle our culture encourages and reinforces. Many of us actually wear our fast-paced schedule and hurried spirit as a badge of honor of our great commitment to our work and the organization we serve. Yet an overextended schedule and a hurried life actually reflect our own self-importance and spiritual impoverishment. Eliminating a hurried, distracted spirit requires intentionality and courage, deliberately slowing our pace, building more margin into our daily schedules, and embracing a more relationally rich, attentive life that enjoys the presence of God and community. Love for God and others seldom flourishes in a hurried existence. A hurried life is inevitably a suffocating, lonely, and joyless life that puts us on the path of burnout.

Slowing Down

Slowing down our lifestyle means saying no more often, to both people and opportunities. This means saying no to many good things and good people. We often hear that good is the enemy of great, and how true that is in proper self-care. As finite creatures we all have limits. Do we see those limits as barriers or as God-given gifts?[12] Our limitations are gifts that allow us to push back the alluring seduction of the fear of missing out and the deception that we can do it all and have it all if we just increase our pace, if we just cram more into our overstuffed, overscheduled lives. It is easy to have our to-do lists but not so easy to have our not-to-do lists.

One of the common conversations my wife and I have as we seek to navigate a healthy, flourishing life in the midst of many demands, unrealistic expectations, and good opportunities is to ask the question, What do we need to eliminate? Where do we need to concentrate? Many of us have way too many to-do lists and too few not-to-do lists. We need to learn to say no so we can say yes to the most important relationships and stewardships of our lives. Paul's admonition to the Thessalonian Christians is often overlooked, to our own impoverishment. Paul's language is fascinating: "Make it your ambition to lead a quiet life" (1 Thess. 4:11 NASB). We don't often equate proper ambition with living a quiet life. Yet that is where Paul places the emphasis. Quiet is not about extroversion or introversion; rather, it means lowering the distractive noise in our life as well as limiting the pace of our lives and embracing a sustainable rhythm. It is often said that life is a marathon and not a sprint. If we are running a marathon and we don't establish a sustainable pace for a long obedience in the same direction, burnout is inescapable. It is just a matter of time. Your pace matters, and so do your lifestyle patterns.

What Are Your Patterns?

Humans are patterned creatures. Patterns are repeatable and consistent ways we do life on a daily or weekly basis, whether that is the route we take to work, when we shop, or where we sit in church. The question is, Do these patterns or habits promote our flourishing or lead us down the path of burnout? We could discuss any number of patterns, but let me highlight three: Sabbath, sleep, and seasons.

What Is Your Sabbath Pattern?

Woven into God's original creation design is a weekly rhythm of work and rest. As Genesis 2 states, God himself rested after he had completed his work, and he blessed and set apart the day of rest.[13] I grew up in a faith context that did not practice weekly Sabbath. My faith tradition overreacted and had an impoverished view of Sabbath, regarding it as an outdated Old Testament ritual filled with arcane restrictions rather than a timeless gift anchored in creation. Tragically, the good baby of Sabbath was thrown out with the dirty legalistic bathwater.

In Genesis we observe that the regular rhythm of Sabbath rest is a godly thing. It is at the heart of the "with God" life, nurturing a deepening relational intimacy. Sabbath rest is God's great gift to us and to his creation. It is a delight, the climax of the week rather than merely the end of an exhausting week. God had all this in mind when including the Sabbath as an integral part of the Ten Commandments. In fact, it is the most expansive commandment. In the fourth commandment we are given a beautiful weekly rhythm and ratio of six to one, where the importance of both work and rest is emphasized.[14] We take seriously the command not to steal or commit adultery, but do we take the command to honor the Sabbath seriously? And if our work takes place on Sunday, finding another day of the week for Sabbath may be difficult, but it is still essential. Abraham Heschel puts it this way: "The Sabbath is not for the sake of the weekdays, the weekdays are for the sake of the Sabbath. It is not an interlude, but the climax of living."[15]

Heschel saw the Sabbath as a delight to the soul and the body as well as a marking of time. He writes, "The meaning of the Sabbath is to celebrate time rather than space. Six days a week we live under the tyranny of things of space; on the Sabbath we try to become attuned to *holiness in time*. It is a day on which we are called upon to share in what is eternal in time, to turn from the results of creation to the mystery of creation; from the world of creation to the creation of the world."[16] The Sabbath is not only for the most devout or super-spiritual; it is for everyone. The weekly Sabbath rhythm is an unhurried and undistracted time for nurturing relationships with God and others. In Sabbath, we are wise to intentionally disconnect from our often overly saturated digital lives, for Sabbath is a time for embodied play and physical activity. In Sabbath rest, we breathe in life-giving beauty for soul and body. We renew our trust in God for his provision for all of life and embrace life-giving patterns, as expressed in the book *Towards Rest*:

> Our souls yearn for us to lay down our tools and toil, and to experience the simple lightness and joys of play. Indeed, play is an antidote to burnout. When we play, we release what was never ours to hold. Our bodies exhale the tensions that bind us. We lay down our defenses and day planners, reborn into the living hope of Christ. In play, we refuse the urges to capitalize, monetize or produce with our time, gifts, and hobbies. In play, we honor our inner child—the one who welcomes Jesus' sacred invitation to rest with him.[17]

It is God's joyous delight to see us participate in Sabbath rest. Do we acknowledge the healing work in each of our lives that God chooses to do only when we rest? Building into our week a Sabbath day fuels our joy, deepens our relationships, and builds greater resilience in our lives—resilience needed to face the many life-draining, anxiety-producing circumstances that we face throughout the week. One of the best preventers of burnout is a weekly Sabbath day. When I encounter someone facing burnout, often there is lack of the Sabbath pattern in their life. What is your Sabbath pattern?

What Is Your Sleep Pattern?

The Bible emphasizes the importance and goodness of sleep. The psalmist writes, "In peace I will both lie down and sleep; for you alone, O LORD, make me dwell in safety" (Ps. 4:8 ESV). When it comes to human flourishing, vocational satisfaction and effectiveness, relational health, and overall well-being, consistent patterns of sleep are vitally important. It has often been said that fatigue makes cowards of us all, but a poor sleep pattern will put us on the path to burnout.

Our sleep patterns reveal much about our internal world and lifestyle. Perhaps you have had the experience of waking up in the middle of the night, your heart, mind, and body all erupting in anxiety as you wrestle with decisions you need to make, difficult relationships that seem irreconcilable, and uncertainties in your physical or mental health or your finances. If we are having regular 3:00 a.m. wake-up calls of anxiety and worry, they may well be warning signs of burnout. Disrupted sleep patterns can point to unfinished business that requires healing.

The church I serve now takes sleep as an important aspect of equipping people in discipleship and spiritual formation. We offer a seminar on sleep, during which a doctor in our congregation who specializes in sleep shares insight about the essential importance of regular and adequate sleep for well-being. Let me recount a few practical tips she has shared. First, there is a relationship between good sleep and regular physical exercise. Daily exercise has multiple benefits, and good sleep is one of them. What is your physical exercise pattern? Second, avoid caffeine in the afternoon and evening and create a regular presleep routine, including a consistent time you go to bed and when you get up. Third, stay away from screens and your phone prior to bedtime. The light of the screen and the stimulation of apps affect melatonin and hinder good sleep. Keep your phone and computer screens out of your bedroom. Keep all work out of your bedroom. Your body has memory, and it will function best when that bedroom space is associated with sleep. How are you sleeping? What is your sleep pattern?

What Is Your Seasonal Pattern?

Many of us live in places and climates with distinct seasonal changes. We wisely adjust to the season with its specific temperature, weather patterns, and length of days. In a similar manner, the resilient person lives wisely into their present season of life. A new season of life will necessitate making changes from the rhythms and patterns of the previous season. I remember hearing an organizational leader once say that we live the first thirty years of our life on adrenaline and the next forty years on wisdom. Are you living on adrenaline or wisdom? Wisdom is always needed, even more so as you move through subsequent seasons of your life. Wisdom will help guide you into doing more of the necessary things rather than just doing more things. It will align your gifts and energy with your job fit. An insightful vocational coach has been essential for me to align my gifts with my work as well as to make necessary adjustments in new seasons of life.

Burnout often happens when we have a misalignment between our gifts and roles but also when we do not make the necessary lifestyle adjustments that new seasons require. Whether you are single or married needs to be considered when it comes to pacing and life patterns. If you and your spouse have young children, your daily and weekly rhythms will be noticeably different from the rhythms of a family with teenagers. If you have adult children or are entering a season of an empty nest or retirement, patterns will change. And though they may look different, in every season you need to embrace yearly vacations and, if possible, some form of extended sabbatical every few years. Pace matters. Patterns matter. People also matter.

Who Are Your People?

In our workplaces we often encounter and serve people, whether they are customers or colleagues, who drain us. Whether we are more extroverted or introverted, we need to be intentional in pursuing close relationships with a handful of life-giving people. Curt Thompson is a practicing psychiatrist who focuses on Christian faith and its intersection with interpersonal neurobiology. He points to isolation and loneliness as a major factor in burnout. Thompson writes, "We know the brain can do a lot of really hard things for a long time as long as it doesn't have to do them by itself. We only develop greater resilience when we are deeply emotionally connected to people."[18] Interpersonal neurobiology and our own experience tell us we can confront virtually anything if we are not alone in facing it.

We were created to flourish within relationally rich community. One correlation of burnout is the increasing spike in isolation and loneliness. Many of us are digitally connected to hundreds of people but are intimately known by very few. We are quick to move away from friends and family for a job opportunity, leaving us isolated from support. The pandemic had a chilling effect on in-person gatherings and led to widespread loneliness and mental health issues. All this points to an important truth: we cannot flourish or heal without community. Jason Shen, an executive coach who works with leaders, notes that the habit he sees in his most resilient clients is their ability to intentionally shift their stress response from a "fight or flight response" to a "tend and befriend response."[19] A "tend and befriend response" focuses on reaching out to one's social connections and caring for others. Close friends and community are essential parts of a flourishing life. We cannot do life alone. Who are you doing life with?

We need a few close friends we know deeply and who know us deeply—friends who are proximate to us, who will not walk out of the room on us when we share our joys, fears, and sorrows with vulnerability and transparency. To truly flourish in our life and work, we need close friends who will be there for us no matter what. Those we truly know and with whom we are truly known—the people we do life with. Do you have friends like that in your life? Are you being a friend like that for a handful of other people? Who in your life do you share your soul with, who will receive you like Jesus does with unconditional acceptance and a gentle, humble heart (Matt. 11:28–30)?

Dan Siegel, a psychiatrist and a leader in interpersonal neurobiology, makes the persuasive point that we all need to relationally experience what he calls the four *S*'s. We all need to experience feeling seen, safe, secure, and soothed in our close relationships.[20] We flourish when we have relationships of empathy and life-giving connection with others. One of our callings in close friendships is to undo the aloneness that others inevitably experience in their life. The good news in regard to the peril of burnout is we can avoid it if we have this kind of close-knit relational community. Even amid life's greatest disappointments, pains, stresses, and heartaches, we can truly flourish.

Your Four Quarters

My wife is a clinically licensed professional counselor. She underscores the importance of the currency of community. She and others in the mental health profession sometimes say that we have one hundred relational pennies. Our hundred pennies are people whose names we know and to whom we have some relational contact. In addition, many of us have ten relational dimes. These are the people we would deem good friends who we hang out with in our workplace, at athletic games, or in some area of common community interest. What is often missing, yet essential for our flourishing, are four relational quarters. Our four quarters are those very close friends we can tell our stories to without judgment or shame—close friends who we can be completely vulnerable with and who we do life with. The four relational quarters will not walk out of the room on us and will always be there for us no matter what. These individuals want to know us more fully, and this is experienced reciprocally. Our four quarters will be there for us in our highest highs and our lowest lows. Who are your four quarters?

If it is difficult to answer that question, begin to more intentionally pursue a few four quarter friendships. Your four quarters may or may not change throughout your life, but they are vital to your flourishing and resilience. A major consideration would be local church commitment and involvement. God designed the local church community for your flourishing. A local faith community is to be a primary place where those four relational quarters are found and nourished. When I meet with someone on the verge of burnout or in the midst of it, I often discover a lack of authentic local church community.[21] Where are you today? Are you on the path to flourishing or the path to burning out? What kind of culture are you nurturing in your workplace? What steps do you need to take right now that will help you avoid burnout and experience greater resilience?

It is common to focus on how burnout harms us and others, but we often fail to reflect on the opportunity cost of burnout—the good things in life that we miss because we're so tired. Burnout robs us of the joyful and creative life of flourishing God designed and wants for us. C. S. Lewis had a lifestyle pattern that included walking in nature outside two hours a day. Lewis thought and wrote a good deal on this pursuit of joy, writing that "joy is the serious business of heaven."[22] As hopeful as that sounds, we don't have to wait until eternity to experience joy. In our apprenticeship with Jesus, the joy of a flourishing life is available to us here and now. So where are you? What is your heart saying to you? Are you experiencing numbing weariness, fatigue, loneliness, lack of creativity, increased negativity, irritability, a loss of connection to God and others? Could now be the time for needed change in your life? There is no better time than now to make some midcourse corrections. Perhaps the cry of your heart is, "Help!" Take the next step. Enlist a close wise friend or a skilled professional to help set you on a trajectory of greater wholeness and flourishing. Make the necessary adjustments now before burnout stops you in your tracks.

A Prayer for God's Strength

God, hear my cry; pay attention to my prayer. I call to you from the ends of the earth when my heart is without strength. Lead me to a rock that is high above me, for you have been a refuge for me, a strong tower in the face of the enemy. I will dwell in your tent forever and take refuge under the shelter of your wings. Selah. (Ps. 61:1–4)

Questions for Reflection and Discussion

Read the remarkable and inspiring story of Elijah in 1 Kings 19:1–18.

- What observations do you make about Elijah's workplace burnout?
- What contributed to Elijah's burnout?
- What made it possible for Elijah to move from the black hole of burnout to a hopeful buoyancy in his work?
- C. S. Lewis once said, "Never, in peace or war, commit your virtue or your happiness to the future. Happy work is best done by the man who takes his long-term plans somewhat lightly and works from moment to moment 'as to the Lord.' It is only our *daily* bread that we are encouraged to ask for. The present is the only time in which any duty can be done or any grace received."[23] Do you have the capacity for this kind of "happy work," given your pace and patterns?
- Who in your life do you share your soul with, who will receive you like Jesus does with unconditional acceptance and a gentle, humble heart? If you don't have anyone like that, how can you find someone?

9

The Changing
Seasons of Work

> For everything there is a season, and a time for every matter
> under heaven.
>
> —Ecclesiastes 3:1 ESV

Growing up in the Midwest, each year I experienced the changes of
the seasons: from the cold, leafless winters; to the early daffodils of
spring; to the hot, long days of summer; to the cool, colorful foliage
of fall, each season had its high and low points, and I learned that
adjustments needed to be made along the way.

The changing of the seasons has been an instructive rubric
through which I increasingly see how life itself and the work we
are called to do emerges and develops with its corresponding possibilities and passions, its creation rhythms of productive activity
and contemplative rest.

For the ancient writer of Ecclesiastes, there was a season for
everything. Grasping the seasonality of God's creation design was

understood as an essential component of the wise and flourishing life. If we are going to live wisely in our daily work, knowing the various seasons of work and cultivating self-awareness is essential. Bringing God's story into our work story means faithfully embracing the changing seasons and rhythms of our lives and callings. As followers of Jesus, our callings are multifaceted and transcend any job we may have, but a vital aspect of our calling is our job. Living a God-honoring life will for most of us involve making a God-honoring living. This will include pursuing and navigating a career path.

The idea of a career is a helpful way to describe the changing seasons of work. The word "career" is often used to refer to white-collar professions or occupations, but it also encompasses blue-collar trades. We can have careers as lawyers, teachers, or plumbers. In most cases careers frame what we do to make a living—that is, the economic engine needed for us to provide for our needs as virtuous actors in a modern advanced economy. Our careers can be quite stable over time or they can radically change throughout our life. Career dynamism is becoming more the normative experience in our Monday worlds. Researcher Vernon Zunker emphasizes the instability emerging in the modern workplace: "Now at the beginning of the twenty-first century, workers have voiced their complaints about how the changing nature of work does not offer them the opportunity of a lifetime job."[1] While this change may offer less job security than in the past, it also opens the door for new career possibilities.[2]

My career story began with my first job as a crew member of a maintenance team at a local golf course. My next job was serving at and then managing a fast-food restaurant. Following college, I worked for a national nonprofit that focused on university students. After I completed graduate school, I became an ordained member of the clergy. For over three decades I have worked for a local church. In addition to my work with the church, I have also worked for a national nonprofit aimed at clergy development and church health.

My career trajectory has led me to work with a literary agent and publishing companies. My career path has reflected the dynamic of change, the necessity of personal growth, and the changing seasons of a career developing over a lifetime.

Wherever you find yourself in your career path, you can anticipate significant change, and this means you will need wisdom to guide you. The writer of Proverbs speaks a great deal about how wisdom is needed in our work, emphasizing themes of diligent work and virtuous workplace ethics. We are reminded that wisdom is gained from a posture of teachability, learning from wise people who have walked the path before us. In Proverbs we read, "The way of a fool is right in his own eyes, but a person who listens to advice is wise" (12:15 NASB), "Listen to advice and accept instruction, that you may gain wisdom in the future" (19:20 ESV), and "Whoever walks with the wise becomes wise, but the companion of fools will suffer harm" (13:20 ESV). The practical skill of daily living flows through multiple relational tributaries, with great benefit attained from many wise counselors: "Without counsel plans fail, but with many advisers they succeed" (15:22 ESV).

The good news is that there is not only wisdom available to us but also good research pertaining to career fit, satisfaction, and effectiveness. An increasing number of career experts offer a variety of theories that shape our understanding of the guiding factors in the career choice process, including personalities, innate traits, gifting, and social contexts. Vernon Zunker helpfully summarizes current career choice theories: "The processes involved in making a career choice have been addressed by career development theories that include a trait-oriented approach, a social learning and cognitive approach, a lifelong development approach, and a person-in-environment perspective."[3]

We must also keep in mind throughout our career journey that supernatural wisdom is available for every follower of Jesus. The New Testament writer James invites us to pray for wisdom, knowing that God generously grants it to those who ask him (James 1:5).

Career and work wisdom is available to us if we embrace a teachable and prayerful spirit, knowing that our Good Shepherd cares about our career and is always with us to guide us and lead us (Ps. 23).

Decade Thinking

When navigating both life and careers, think not primarily in years but in decades. Our first decade (years one to ten) is one of memories, when so much of our personalities and relational attachment patterns are formed. Our second decade (eleven to twenty) is characterized by mischief highlighted in the turbulent teens, when exploration, identity, early job experience, and often risky behaviors are prevalent. Our third decade is a decade of the majors (twenty-one to thirty). During this time many of the major decisions, including education choices, geographical preferences, early career formation, significant relationships, and housing decisions put us on a trajectory on which once seemingly endless career possibilities become more limited. Our fourth decade (thirty-one to forty) is marked by mastery. This is a time of increased workplace skill, greater responsibility, promotion opportunity, and increased earning potential. Our fifth decade (forty-one to fifty) is one of multiplication. This decade reveals growing influence of our workplace mastery and greater influence in our broader career field. The workplace mastery gained in the earlier decades is now sought out by other individuals and organizations. New doors open and new career and entrepreneurial possibilities begin to emerge. Our sixth through our eighth decades (fifty-one to eighty) are the decades of mentoring, where generativity to younger generations reaches its zenith. Effectively navigating the rhythms of each decade allows us to move successfully and seamlessly to the stage of influence. However, a decade of stagnation will disrupt and impede the growth process and minimize new career opportunities in the emerging decades.

If we are going to be wise in our career pursuits, we should not only think in terms of decades but also recognize what season we find ourselves in today. Where are you now located in your career journey? Stages of life and seasons of a career are closely linked. Jeff Haanen proposes a threefold framework around life stages: young adulthood, midlife, and older adulthood. He writes, "In young adulthood, we learn to take responsibility for our lives. In midlife, the challenge is to accept ourselves for who we are, for better or worse. Older adulthood (retirement) is a season of letting go in order to bless and offer wisdom to a coming generation."[4] I find it helpful to think of career journeys in three seasons: the early years of young adulthood, the maturing years of midlife, and the retirement years of older adulthood. I liken these to the season of formation, the season of maturation, and the season of retirement.

The Season of Career Formation

I have had the joy of knowing her since she was a bubbly young girl. Emma Green is now a bright, talented, engaging, and vivacious young woman who completed her undergraduate college degree from an acclaimed Christian college outside Chicago. At a Christmas dinner hosted by her parents in Kansas City, I sat across from Emma, who had just returned for the holidays from her new home in Boston. Over dinner we had a conversation around her early career experience. Following college, Emma took a job serving the scheduling and administrative needs of a group of tenured professors ensconced in an esteemed academic institution. Emma described her move to Boston with great energy and voiced her excitement about the steep learning curve she was now on as she navigated a new world of emerging adulthood. Emma found herself working harder than she envisioned yet also enjoying it more than she imagined. The new city she was exploring, the new church community she had found, the rich learning environment of her job, and the many amazing people she was meeting all spoke to me about the richness and possibility of the early stage of career formation. Emma shared with me the excitement of her new world and how her job was teaching her more about herself. She was learning more about who she is, what she loves to do, and what might be ahead in her career future.

Regardless of the particularities of our early jobs, Emma's work experience embodies the season of career formation. While we need discernment in every season of our career, it is vitally important during career formation. In this season we are asking, What work/career should I pursue? When I interact with followers of Jesus in this early season, the question I hear most often is, *How do I figure out what God is calling me to do?* This season is one of vital self-discovery and peak discernment where significant thought, prayer, and effort must be expended. William Placher helps us keep in mind God's sovereignty over our career path: "To believe that a wise and good God is in charge of things implies that there is a fit between things that need doing and the person I am meant to be."[5]

Bryan Dik is a vocational psychologist who has thought a great deal about the necessity of wise exploration in the career-formation stage. He wisely writes, "Making career choices is like detective work. It requires gathering good information (e.g., about one's gifts and about various career paths), envisioning different possibilities, and consulting with trusted advisors to identify possible blind spots. It involves looking for consistencies that converge across multiple data sources. It takes patience, persistence, effort and wisdom."[6] Putting on our Sherlock Holmes hat, how do we go about figuring out our work calling, our career fit? What should we be attentive to and what considerations are most important? The most important aspect of career exploration is embracing a trusting posture of prayer, knowing that God not only is with us in our present work but is also ahead of us in our future work. We can be confident that a sovereign God who knew us before we were born, who can count every hair on our head, who has numbered our days has a plan for our work lives to bring glory to him and to contribute to others.[7] How has God designed you? How are you wired? What gifts and talents has God given you that you need to steward and then employ in serving others in your career path? The apostle Peter speaks of the stewardship of our gifting when he writes, "Each of you should use whatever gift you have received to serve others, as faithful stewards of God's grace in its various forms" (1 Pet. 4:10 NIV).

Growing up in a large family with three really smart brothers, I quickly realized that I was not gifted like them. My brothers were amazingly skilled with their hands. They could design and build anything. I could build nothing. When I was invited to assist them in a building project, my duties were mostly restricted to running errands for supplies or refilling coffee mugs. Realizing my deficiencies was at first discouraging, yet as I continued to gain greater self-awareness, I began to realize God had designed me with another kind of giftedness. I had a gift for ideas, and while I could not design or build buildings, I could design and build organizations. I had a knack for designing organizational culture. I also had an entrepreneurial gift, the ability to start things from a mere concept and bring them to concrete reality.

Growing in the understanding of and implications of our giftedness is highly important in career discernment and formation. My friend Bill Hendricks has devoted much of his career to assisting others in career discernment. Bill defines giftedness this way: "Giftedness is the unique way in which you function. It's a set of inborn core strengths and natural motivation you instinctively and consistently use to do things that you find satisfying and productive. Giftedness is not just what you can do but what you are born to do, enjoy doing and do well."[8] Bill makes the case that many things change in life over the years, but our essential giftedness does not change. Perhaps more important, our core motivations are a stable factor over the course of a lifetime. In his career coaching, Bill helpfully employs a narrative approach that helps people see where their motivational aptitudes repeatedly surface in their unfolding life and work story.[9] When we are working outside our giftedness, we can find ourselves on the path to burnout. Bill puts it well: "When you're working at a job that doesn't fit you, you end up hating life."[10]

We don't always find that career sweet spot, but if and when we do, we have the satisfying sense that this is what God has made us to do, that we were created for this work and this moment. Frederick Buechner captures this career ideal: "God calls you to the kind of work that you need most to do, and that the world most needs to have done. . . . The place God calls you is the place where your deep gladness and the world's deep hunger meets."[11]

What if we are not in an ideal career environment? This is often the case in the season of career formation and may be our experience throughout our career. Let me encourage you that many in today's dynamic job market do not stay in the same job for long periods of time. Let me also remind you that sometimes we learn what we are about when we work in areas that inform us what we are *not* about. Our giftedness can be recognized not only when we do things well but also when we do things poorly or when we don't have a great job fit. Wherever we are in our career, even if it is not a great fit, it is never wasted by God. Some of our most profound spiritual and personal formation takes place in contexts of difficulties, hardships, and even failures (Rom. 5:3–5). Failure in our careers is one of our most insightful teachers and is often the back door to better job fit, greater job satisfaction, and workplace effectiveness.

If you are in a season of career formation, let me suggest a few practical considerations. If you know someone who is doing work effectively that you think you might be called to do, take the initiative to reach out to them. Inquire about what their work is like and, if possible, shadow them for a day. Find out what prepared them to be effective in their line of work. Ask what education and experience were needed on their career journey. As you seek the career God is calling you to do, create a prayer journal in which you take the necessary unhurried time to ask several discernment questions: What do I enjoy doing? What experiences have shaped me? What circumstances surround me? What career opportunities exist and may be presenting themselves to me?[12] While we are wise to prayerfully plan in the career-formation season, the most important thing is being faithful each and every day where God has presently called us to serve him, trusting that he will guide us. Wisdom invites us to trust in the Lord with all our heart, to acknowledge him in all our ways, and to have confidence that he will direct our paths (Prov. 3:5–6).

The Season of Career Maturation

The early years of career formation transition to the middle years of career maturation. While the season of formation often focuses on figuring out what God has called us to do, the season of maturation focuses on how to keep growing and gaining mastery in our workplace skill. The writer of Proverbs captures well the season of career maturation: "Do you see a man skillful in his work? He will stand before kings; he will not stand before obscure men" (Prov. 22:29 ESV). The middle years might well be called the mastery years, where increased career skill is forged in the rich learning context of extensive workplace experience. Many trade careers like plumbers, mechanics, carpenters, and electricians reflect this career maturation stage by adding the title of master to a worker's job title, which brings with it increasing prestige and greater compensation. Other careers often reflect this maturation stage with the addition of new graduate-level degrees and advanced certifications.

My wife and I have a few skilled professionals who help us maintain our home. A Kansas City–based company we have utilized for many years services our HVAC equipment. When their technicians come to our door, their identification badge informs us of not only their name but also their tenure with the company and how many years of experience they have, including their skill-level certification. For some, their identification badge lists the level of mastery they have achieved over the years. It is not uncommon for technicians who have achieved a mastery level to be accompanied by an apprentice technician whose early career stage has not yet provided enough experience to do the job alone.

In the middle years of career mastery, we continue growing in our skills and knowledge and often assume a teaching role for those earlier in their career. Matt Earnest is in the middle mastery years of his career as a cardiologist. Matt, who describes himself as a high-tech plumber, works in a teaching hospital where a cadre of medical students, residents, and fellows learn from him as they do heart procedures together. Matt invited me to shadow him at his workplace, where I observed firsthand not only his skill mastery but also his active mentoring of younger physicians. Matt shares his mastery with others, but as he works and teaches others, he also continues to deepen his own knowledge and skill.

In the middle years of our careers, we can either continue to grow or stagnate. I have found it helpful to draw on the insight of a learning model made popular by Abraham Maslow.[13] This model postulates four essential stages of learning that we progress through on our way from ignorance to mastery. The first stage is unconscious incompetence. Simply put, at this stage we don't know that we don't know. We live in blissful ignorance. Our great need in this first stage is to be exposed to reality, where our deficit of knowing and skill cannot be hidden or rationalized. The bubble of our ignorance is burst.

The second stage, conscious incompetence, now emerges. At this stage of learning, we now know that we don't know. With this realization is often the shattering of false confidence. When we realize that we truly don't know, we have the choice to become teachable and grow or remain willfully ignorant. We now have the golden opportunity to embrace a journey of disciplined learning, unlearning and relearning through increased propositional information and the tacit knowledge that comes from apprenticeships with those who have achieved the next stage of learning.

The third stage is conscious competence. At this stage of learning we now know that we know what we're doing. This stage is often described as growing mastery. Our learning and skill attainment have now reached a level where we no longer need direct assistance from others to excel. More people know us as a growing expert in our field. With this expertise we are invited into higher levels of leadership and responsibility. Often we are also invited into a smaller industry or vocational career circle, exploring new frontiers of knowledge. We now have the choice to coast in our level-three mastery or remain highly disciplined by continuing to stay curious, exploring higher competencies, and going where few have gone before us.

If we continue to grow in the third stage of learning, at some point the fourth and final stage of learning emerges: unconscious competence. In this stage, we don't consciously know how much we know. The learning and skill we have attained has now become second nature to us. Performing a skill or accessing knowledge is virtually effortless and often without focused thought. The fourth learning stage is rarefied air. Few ever achieve this level of skill or knowledge. At the fourth level comes the peril of prideful isolation and self-indulgence rather than stewarding our high-level competence in order to mentor others and serve the common good.

We can apply these four levels to the process of learning a musical instrument, to the routine of a gymnast on the balance beam, or to our careers. In my own career, I've used the four-level learning model in my own skill development and have come alongside others to help them reach the next level of mastery. One skill I have had to develop the most is public speaking. When I look back at my early years of speaking, my skill level was mediocre at best, but over time with coaching, consistent discipline, preparation, and lots of practice, I have moved through levels one and two and have experienced the joy of achieving significant mastery.

If you find yourself in the career stage of maturation or are moving in that direction, what level of learning best describes your current development? What education, experience, or exposure will help you get to the next level of learning and skill attainment? Who in the level of learning ahead of you can assist you to get to the next level? In the season of career maturation, it is important to keep growing in terms of both our skills and who we are becoming.

While the middle years of career mastery are filled with great promise, they can also be perilous. The internal insecurities we feel, and the external expectations often placed on us, can lead us to neglect our primary relationship with God and those closest to us. The idol of workaholism can be masked in our pursuit of career advancement and skill attainment. We must always be vigilant against the siren song of career success that hijacks our primary identity as beloved children of God. If God calls us to marriage and the raising of children, navigating competing demands of home and work will require continual evaluation, recalibration, and accountability. At times we will need to say no to our career in order to say yes to our family. For example, a lawyer in an early career season adopts two children and chooses to delay that career for fifteen years only to return to the workplace and experience an amazing career path that continues until age seventy.

The middle years of career mastery will also require ongoing calling and career reassessment. In each season we can be confident that our Good Shepherd will be with us, guide us, protect us, and keep us close to his heart.

Over breakfast one day, one of my early mentors looked at me and with a heavy heart described many young pastors he knew who had ruined their family and health to be more successful in their work. This seasoned sage gave me two words of advice that I have held close to my heart. He said, "Never lose your family over your work, and always love where you go home at night. Make your home a refuge from the world." This man's wisdom has stayed with me when career ambition, work demands, or success was wooing my heart away from what is most important.

Making the Most of Unemployment

Another formidable challenge we can face in any season of work is unemployment. Being out of a job may have been precipitated by broader economic circumstances or our own lack of productivity or poor fit. We may find ourselves out of work because we resigned, were terminated, or experienced a company's workforce-reduction decision. However unemployment strikes us, it has an immediate impact on our emotional and financial well-being. Our work is often closely tied to our sense of self-worth, and when we lose our job we can feel a great deal of worthlessness and self-doubt. Fear and worry can rob us of a good night's sleep. We also can find ourselves in an energy-zapping hole of bitterness and discouragement. We may even blame God for what has happened to us. When we find ourselves unemployed, how do we make the most of it?

While looking back and assessing what we can learn from our previous work experience may be helpful, our primary energy should be focused on navigating the road ahead of us. We can have confidence that our sovereign God is in control of our lives and circumstances and that he will guide and provide for us as we walk in faith.

When we trust God, we can take positive steps forward. First, create a working schedule for your life. In many cases securing employment is a full-time job in itself, so structure your day and week accordingly. Second, get in a disciplined rhythm that includes good eating practices, physical exercise, and spiritual-formation activities. Though your finances may be limited, include some fun times and recreation opportunities as well. Also look for opportunities to volunteer and help others. Perhaps give a few hours each week to volunteer at a local Habitat for Humanity project, assist the hungry and the homeless in your city, or serve your local church in some way. Third, don't put off making the practical financial adjustments in your budget that are prudent with your income reduction. In many cases this will mean a significant reduction in your spending and making room for a simplified lifestyle. Avoid taking on credit card or consumer debt if possible. Fourth, find a support group of others who are also looking for a job. You will find encouragement that you are not the only one facing the challenges of unemployment, new friendships are often forged out of a shared situation, and new job search ideas can emerge. Finally, get out and meet with as many people as possible who may be able to open a door for you or expand your job-hunting network.

Pray hard. Do your homework. Network extensively. Take the initiative. A door will open if you keep asking, keep knocking, and keep seeking.

As a pastor I interact regularly with many who face unexpected unemployment. Though it is challenging, I often see that it is also a positive time of spiritual and personal growth. Many times, new work ideas and new opportunities never considered before present themselves. Unemployment provides a unique time of personal evaluation and career exploration seldom possible while working a full-time job. God often allows one door to be closed in order to guide us to another open door that is a better fit for our vocational calling.

Any extended period of unemployment can be very stressful and challenging. It can easily lead to discouragement and isolation. What do we do when the embers of hope in our hearts seem to be fading? Memorizing and meditating on God's Word fans the flame of hope in our hearts. As a pastor I often write out a prescription for those who come to me and are struggling to stay hopeful in the midst of bleak circumstances. I write down a text of Scripture to be memorized and meditated on three times a day. My primary prescription for a buoyant hope is Psalm 121. I commend it to you.

The Season of Career Retirement

Steve Harvey began his career in a local auto shop. With the mechanical skills he had gained he was soon given the opportunity for an entry-level position in the fleet department of a telecommunications company. This began a forty-seven-year career in the telecom industry during which Steve, a lifelong learner, took college courses, eventually obtaining a bachelor's and master's degree. The majority of Steve's career was spent in the corporate world in a middle management position. Throughout his career, he cultivated his spiritual life and served in various capacities in his local church. As Steve moved from the season of career maturation to the season of career retirement, he spent considerable time in prayerful reflection as to what retirement would mean for him. Now in the season of retirement, Steve has more flexible time for family and travel but still works in a part-time role as my executive assistant. Steve's knowledge and experience are invaluable in helping me navigate the complexities of my work world. Steve would also say his work as an executive assistant keeps him engaged intellectually and encourages him to keep growing and constantly learning. He also mentors and equips others who are preparing for retirement, and he gives leadership to those in our local church who are focusing on the third season of their lives.

Retirement will look different for each one of us as we enter this season with varying physical, emotional, relational, spiritual, and financial realities. No two retirement journeys will be the same. For some, retirement will be the end of our paid work. Others will embrace a partial retirement, cutting back significantly on existing work or embracing some other part-time remunerative work. Because of fewer financial resources, others will delay their retirement in order to bolster their savings. Still others will retire from their jobs for a while, only to return to full-time paid work for an extended period.

If we are going to bring God's story of work into the season of retirement, we will need to recognize that many cultural narratives guiding this season of our life and work are impoverished. A friend of mine humorously summarized the predominant career objective this way: "To work as hard as I can, to save as much as I can, and then sit on my can." While this may be a rather crude way to articulate the aim of retirement, it does capture much of our cultural messaging as an endless vacation. I often hear conversations around retirement focused on having a bucket list. A bucket list contains activities and experiences we desire before kicking the bucket. While the idea of a bucket list isn't necessarily negative, many times it is built on the assumption that we go around only once in life, that this life is all there is, so we have to squeeze as much pleasure out of it as we can before we die. For the follower of Jesus, there is no bucket list that can begin to capture the eternal wonders, experiences, and opportunities available to us in the new heavens and new earth. If we don't get to all that is on our bucket list before our expiration date, there is much more ahead of us.

Cultural narratives about retirement are often very individualized. Retirement is seen as a time to pursue gratifications that have not yet been experienced or have been postponed. The wellness industry appeals to retirees to maintain physical and mental health in aging. The financial industry aggressively markets to those contemplating retirement, eliciting the fear of outliving their money and becoming a burden to others. Jeff Haanen describes a perfect storm for those entering retirement: a growing number of Americans struggle to save enough for retirement, pension plans are underfunded, health-care costs are rising, and Americans are living longer than ever, outstripping their savings.[14]

In addition to motivations of self-indulgence and fear of not having enough or being healthy enough, there's a dearth of cultural narratives that focus on spiritual growth and the beckoning of eternity. In much of our retirement thinking, God's story of work in the latter years of life seems glaringly absent.

God's Story of Retirement

When we examine the Scriptures, we do not find very much about retiring from the work God has called us to do. In what seems to be a special case, Moses gives detailed instructions to the Levites who served in the tabernacle. "The LORD spoke to Moses: 'In regard to the Levites: From twenty-five years old or more, a man enters the service in the work at the tent of meeting. But at fifty years old he is to retire from his service in the work and no longer serve. He may assist his brothers to fulfill responsibilities at the tent of meeting, but he must not do the work. This is how you are to deal with the Levites regarding their duties'" (Num. 8:23–26). Even in Moses's instruction regarding the Levites' mandatory retirement, they are permitted to assist the younger leaders who have now been tasked with leading the Israelites.

While the Bible says little about the season of retirement, it paints a hopeful picture of God's faithfulness to his people throughout their entire lives, encouraging continual spiritual growth and calling for the stewardship of generativity to the emerging generations. The psalmist describes this later season of life: "God, you have taught me from my youth, and I still proclaim your wondrous works. Even while I am old and gray, God, do not abandon me, while I proclaim your power to another generation, your strength to all who are to come" (Ps. 71:17–18).

As we prepare for the season of retirement, a wise approach suggests we carve out significant time for prayerful reflection long before we make this transition. With increased longevity for many, the retirement season has rightly been called the "third third of life." Jeff Haanen helps us to see the dynamic change in the length of the retirement season. "In 1900, the average male could expect to live to age 46 and the average female, age 48. Presently, if you are now 20 you have a 50 percent chance of living to more than 100; if you are 40 you have an even chance of reaching 95; if you are 60, then a 50 percent chance of making 90 or more. Over the last two hundred years, life expectancy has increased at a rate of more than two years every decade. If you retire at age 65, this means that you will have an even chance of living 25 years beyond retirement."[15] Although we don't know the number of our days, we are wise to plan and prepare for the very real possibility of a retirement season of a quarter century.

As followers of Jesus we must keep in mind that we will one day give an account to God for how we have stewarded our time, talent, and treasure throughout all seasons, including retirement.[16] Retirement is not about self-absorption; it is about God-honoring stewardship. How are you going to steward this important season of your life? As we prepare for retirement, we find ourselves in different places and financial circumstances. It is never too early or too late in your career to prepare for the retirement season. Carve out the necessary time to look back at your life and career. Creating a journal can be helpful. What did you or are you now enjoying most in your work? What is life-giving and what is energy-depleting? How does this reflection help you consider the possibilities of contributing in a post-paycheck world? As we ponder the season of retirement, it is important to reflect on questions around identity, friendships, spiritual community, and hope. What is my identity now? Where will I find meaning? Who are my friends? Where is my spiritual community? Can I look to the future with hope? How do I need to adjust my weekly rhythms and recalibrate my life?

While some of us are naturally more inclined to be planners, every one of us needs to do some planning for retirement. Winging it doesn't work very well. So where do we begin? Let me offer some practical steps moving forward. Make it a priority to engage a wise financial planner who embraces your Christian values. Create with your financial professional a retirement plan that includes all facets of retirement, including investment, tax, and philanthropic strategies. Find a legal professional who will help you in estate planning and end-of-life directives. Take your annual physicals seriously and consult your medical professionals regrading healthy lifestyle practices and aging considerations. Engage a pastor or wise Christian friend who will help you think through spiritual growth opportunities and service possibilities within both your local church and the broader community. Read a couple of books on retirement. Take advantage of an increasing number of very helpful resources that assist those preparing for retirement.[17] Preparing for the retirement season is not a solitary endeavor; we need others to come alongside us and share with us the practical wisdom we need for this new season of life.

The Bible speaks of the latter season of our lives as a time of great flourishing and fruitfulness. With great hopefulness, the psalmist declares, "The righteous flourish like the palm tree and grow like a cedar in Lebanon. They are planted in the house of the LORD; they flourish in the courts of our God. They still bear fruit in old age; they are ever full of sap and green, to declare that the LORD is upright; he is my rock, and there is no unrighteousness in him" (Ps. 92:12–15 ESV). In *Aging Matters*, R. Paul Stevens rightly speaks of the priority of continued growth and learning rather than self-centered indulgence and stagnation. He writes, "First, retirees should replace their work mates with another social network. Second, they must rediscover how to play. Third, they must cultivate creativity."[18] Continuing to cultivate our spiritual lives, fostering deepening friendships, seeking opportunities for personal growth, and staying curious can be the true hallmark of retirement.[19] One of the most helpful disciplines in the early weeks and months of retirement is to take an extended sabbatical. This sabbatical allows the quiet and unhurried context to listen carefully to God's still, small voice and to attend to areas of our inner world that need attention as well as to seek his specific direction for the years ahead.

The retirement season is brimming with possibilities for deeper relational growth and also allows retirees to utilize years of life and work experience to invest in the lives of younger generations. This generative mindset and investment often takes the form of developing mutual learning friendships as well as specific mentoring in areas of career expertise and experience. Stevens puts practical flesh on the concept of retirement generativity: "Generativity is about investing in the next generation, mentoring younger people, being creative in work whether voluntary or remunerated, being a blessing to society and the church, being explorers and adventurers."[20]

In the ever-changing seasons of work, may we follow Jesus closely, love his church dearly, and honor him in who we are becoming and in all that we are doing. A fellow student penned words of wisdom in my high school yearbook that have been regular companions of my heart over the years: "A good life is someone to love, something to do, and something to hope for." In every career season, in Jesus's already-but-not-yet kingdom, you have others to love, you have things to do, and you truly have something to hope for.

A Prayer for Fruitfulness

Heavenly Father, thank you for your work in and through the work I have already done. Please show me how to be faithfully present to this season. Grant me wisdom for and fruitfulness in the next season of my work. In Jesus's name, amen.

Questions for Reflection and Discussion

- What are the implications of the season of work you find yourself in now?
- How are you discerning your God-given giftedness in your work?
- Who are your wise vocational counselors? How have you allowed them to speak into your life?
- What cultural narratives of retirement do you need to reexamine?
- In Psalm 90:12, the psalmist encourages us to number our days, that we would have the wisdom needed to flourish in life. How are you taking the psalmist's words to heart?

10

The Changing World of Work

Technology has changed our world so drastically that the biblical character Abraham of 2000 BC would probably have more in common with Abraham Lincoln of the early 1800s than Lincoln would have with us in the twenty-first century.

—John Dyer[1]

Milwaukee has had many nicknames: the Beer Capital, Cream City, and America's Toolbox. Historically, Milwaukee has had a hard-working blue-collar personality, so it is fitting that the Milwaukee School of Engineering has a museum that celebrates the art of work. The Grohmann Museum houses the world's most comprehensive art collection dedicated to the changing world of work. The Man at Work collection displays more than one thousand paintings and sculptures spread across three floors of galleries and a welcoming rooftop sculpture garden.[2]

Visiting the Grohmann was an unforgettable experience. I was struck by its extensive quantity and high artistic quality. Each masterful canvas brushstroke told a compelling story of human work.

Painting after painting portrayed the human experience with emerging tools of technology and an ever-changing workplace, grouped in dedicated vignettes of agriculture, industry, and enterprise. Beautiful works of art captured the bucolic vistas of family members with bare hands and bent backs harvesting a field. Other works welcomed me into the rugged workplaces of railroads, steam engines, internal combustion engines, and efficient assembly lines of the industrial era. More recent art ushered me into the changing workplaces of air-conditioned offices, air travel, public education, telecommunications, and modern medicine. Other exhibits depicted the transformation of the information age with its computerization, miniaturization, internet connectivity, robotics, and convergent phone technology.

The Grohmann is a hidden gem. It portrays how the human story is deeply tied to our work and our workplaces. Seemingly every job imaginable is represented in some way and resonates deeply with our own work experience. The exhibits do not portray the famous or the celebrity but rather celebrate the more commonplace people like you and me who diligently work unseen in their Monday worlds. Whether we are accountants, lawyers, engineers, entrepreneurs, physicians, teachers, chefs, plumbers, or carpenters, we see ourselves on the artist's canvas. With each work of art, we look into a mirror to see who we are and the work we do, with its mundane regularity and its exasperating toil but also with its inspiring satisfaction and image-bearing meaning. Through the lenses of art and history, the Grohmann Museum helps us to see the goodness of work as well as the changing nature of human work, the emerging technological tools of our work, and the differing settings of our workplaces.

If there is one constant in our work worlds, it is change. Over several decades I have encountered a great deal of change in my workplace. I am not sure I could accurately enumerate the number of computers I have had or the many adaptations in the software programs I have needed to learn. Being an information-based worker, much of my research now comes not in the form of a paper book but in a digital format on one of my electronic devices. When I do research, I seldom go to a physical library, because I can access everything I need on the internet from my phone or computer. As a pastor my weekly schedule often now includes as many online meetings as it does in-person meetings. With a few keystrokes I can access our church database and immediately correspond with anyone in our congregation. I can also prepare a sermon, write a blog, or work on a book from any location. The geographic location of my workstation is now much more fluid. When I travel, the tools of my trade come with me.

With emerging technologies, navigating my work in a hyper-connected world also presents new physiological, emotional, and relational challenges. My doctor visits explore increased job-related stress and the importance of nutritious food and an active lifestyle. My annual optometrist appointment increasingly focuses on eye strain and the importance of limiting screen time. A professional work coach now assists me in evaluating my yearly calendar and guides me in navigating the organizations I serve. Change greets me every workday.

Whatever work God has called you to do, you are assuredly encountering lots of change in your workplace. A grocery store clerk who once had constant face-to-face interaction with other humans now focuses more on helping customers use the self-checkout stations. A customer service employee at a rental car company now points customers to a kiosk to complete their online reservation. The auto mechanic deals with more than wrenches, hoses, bolts, and belts—they increasingly need the skills of a computer analyst. Automobiles have become like computers on four wheels. The farmer's tractor provides more than sheer horsepower; it is now a computerized high-tech machine, continually assessing weather and soil conditions, guided in precise detail by a global positioning signal. One of my neighbors mows his lawn with a high-tech robot that slowly and methodically covers his yard without him ever having to lift a finger. Many of the changes impacting our work and influencing our workplaces are tied to changes in technology. An important aspect of our discipleship to Jesus relates to how we think about and navigate technological change.

Technology and God's Work Story

How do all our recent technological changes fit into the biblical story of work? To explore this question, we must return once again to the beginning story of work in the Bible. In Genesis 1:26–27, we read that humans are image bearers of God. As image bearers, we reflect the nature and character of the God who created us. An essential aspect of our created essence and nature is that we have a remarkable creative capacity. We create out of what God has created and join with his ongoing creation in the world. We also read in Genesis 1:28 that we have been given a work mandate to be fruitful, multiply, fill the earth, subdue it, and have dominion. In Genesis 2, Adam's Edenic job description is to "cultivate" and "keep" the garden (2:15 NASB 1995).

In this work mandate, Adam is commissioned to take the raw materials of God's created world—the soil, the water, the trees, the plants, the rocks—imagine with his brain, and create new things from them with his hands. It's as if God gave Adam a bin of Legos and said, "Adam, here you go. Now make something good and beautiful from them. The sky's the limit. Enjoy!"

What does God's creation design for humanity tell us about technology? Technology comprises the material and nonmaterial tools and capacities we create and develop in fulfilling the work mandate, reflecting our image-bearing nature. Foundationally, technology is a gift from God and is a part of our human job description within his work story. John Dyer describes his transforming encounter with God's work story and technology: "As I began to reread the biblical story with technology in mind, I saw things I hadn't noticed before about how deeply God cares about the things we make and how we use them. God's original calling on humanity was to have dominion over all the earth, making things from what he had made, moving humanity . . . from the garden to the city, or more specifically from the garden of Eden (Genesis 2) to the city of heaven (Hebrews 11:16; Revelation 21)."[3]

Dyer rightly reminds us that, when we think about and encounter technological change in our lives and in our workplaces, we need to see it through the clarifying lens of the sweeping biblical story, a story that moves from a pristine garden long ago to a new city that is yet to arrive in the new heavens and new earth. A part of God's story of work now is that we live and work in a broken, sinful world. We and our work have not yet made a full pilgrimage to that sinless city. But is our technology just tools that we use and nothing more? Or is there more we need to understand about technology itself?

Is Technology Neutral?

Sometimes we are tempted to think that the technological tools we develop are neutral. Yet while the technology we create and the work we now do can be aimed at good or evil outcomes, technology itself is not neutral. We shape our tools and our tools shape us. As artifacts of culture, they influence our specific workplace context in ways we might not realize. The technology we create rewires our brains, affecting us physiologically as well as socially. A skilled logger or carpenter using the technology of an axe or a saw will develop hand calluses and stronger upper-body muscles along with very specific neuropathways and muscle memory. A cardiologist using robotic technology to put a stent in a clogged heart artery strengthens neuropathways in her brain and refines her fine motor skills.

In an increasingly digital world, our brains are rewired to process massive amounts of information at nanosecond speed. Neuroscientists remind us of our brain's plasticity, telling us that neurons that fire together wire together. Our encounters with other humans online are processed in certain ways in our brains and affect us differently than face-to-face, flesh-and-blood conversation and community. Our phones help us connect to people and gain information, but they also often distract us, impoverishing our relationships. Screen-driven technology shortens our attention spans, impacts our mental health, and rearranges our lives in ways that often hinder our spiritual formation and flourishing.

When I go to a restaurant, it is not uncommon to observe families or colleagues staring at their phones rather than speaking with one another. Families are wisely embracing the discipline of removing phones and screen devices from the dinner table. More workplaces are declaring staff meetings phone-free zones, where this often disruptive and distractive technology is restricted.

Phone-based and screen-based technology is doing more than simply helping us to communicate; it is also hindering us from forming and maintaining some of our deepest human connections. God's design for human flourishing embraces physical embodiment and attentive eye-to-eye presence. Let's not forget that Jesus the eternal Son of God took on human flesh and in his glorious resurrection had a resurrected body. With his resurrected body, Jesus was present with his disciples and made a breakfast for them (John 21:4–14). Being digitally connected can serve a good purpose and bring a meaningful degree of human connection, but it is not the same as being physically present with others. We live and work in a hyperconnected world, yet ironically we feel an increasing sense of soul-numbing loneliness.

In a digitalizing world, we must become more attentive to how technology has the power to overwhelm us and distract us from cultivating intimacy with God and fostering meaningful relationships with others. Technology also brings with it a set of values, and this requires users of technology to think critically about these tools, examining them through the clarifying lens of the biblical story and biblical ethics. Technology increasingly offers us greater efficiencies and new freedoms, but the inconvenient truth is it can also impoverish and enslave us. It can be programmed by motivated companies with algorithms designed to addict its users to ever-increasing amount of screen time at the expense of live, human relationships. Excessive digital use can promote a lifestyle of disembodiment that is shallow, sedentary, and excessively solitary. Often asynchronous, a digital life can promote a consumption mindset rather than a connection mindset, which often follows us into our embodied relationships.

Technological innovation gives us increased power to do more and more things, but it doesn't offer us the ethical guidance of whether we should do what technology enables us to do. Just because we can employ technology in a particular way doesn't mean we should. Like any gift of God, technology can be ill purposed, misguided, and misused. Technology can be employed for great good or great evil. The same technology developed to split the atom can bring electrical power to millions of homes but also can be used in atomic bombs to destroy millions of people. The same technology can either save or terminate an unborn child's life.

Dyer brings a clarifying gospel perspective on technology. He points out technology's role in the cruel death of Jesus our Savior, who rescues us and will one day redeem all things: "At one end of this story is a pristine garden prepared by God for humankind to develop and transform. At the other end is a glorious, heavenly city full of human creations, art, and technology. At the center is our Savior Jesus Christ crucified on a cross, the most horrific of all technological distortions, built by transforming a tree from the natural world into a tool of death. Yet in his resurrection, Christ redeemed even that tool, transforming it into our symbol of faith that eternally portrays his power over death and sin."[4]

We need to think critically when adopting technologies, knowing that the tools we use can be positively formational or can disfigure us as image bearers of God. These technologies are now entrusted to our stewardship and are to be exercised responsibly and excellently under God's kingdom reign. This means we need to be aware of technology's potential for good and evil as well as the potential unintended consequences that misalign with God's story of work and desire for human flourishing. Most important, as apprentices of Jesus we must guard our hearts from technology's idolatrous wooing.

In Technology We Trust?

It is easy to think of idols as something reserved for ancient superstitious people who made statues of stone and then bowed before them in some religious ritual. Yet an idol is anything in our lives that we make ultimate instead of God. Idols are God substitutes. They are what we truly trust for security, significance, meaning, and connection. For most of us in the modern world, idols take a different form than they did for the ancients, yet there are also similarities when it comes to technology.

Think with me about the work story of the tower of Babel in Genesis 11. These ancient people gather together and use their latest technology to build an amazing city. We read, "Then they said, 'Come let us build ourselves a city and a tower with its top in the heavens, and let us make a name for ourselves'" (Gen. 11:4 ESV). At first glance it may seem like these people are fulfilling God's mandate to subdue the earth and have dominion. Yet a closer look reveals the misguided motivation for this massive building project. Of particular importance is where their trust was anchored. They trusted not in God but rather in their technological tools that offered them a utopian dream, a seductive mirage of a flourishing life apart from God. The tower of Babel is a sobering picture of the idolatry of human technology.

We might refer to the idolatry of technology as "technism," which is a utopian belief that technology is humanity's great savior, a replacement for God offering us true happiness and transcendence. In a high-tech world, where it may seem we can solve every problem and have everything under control, the one true Creator God becomes unnecessary and irrelevant. We can seek relational connectivity through our phones, watches, and computers that demand our attention by notifications that pull us away from real people right in front of us. Our social media presence can define our self-worth, self-esteem, and mood. As technology makes more and more of life easy and seemingly under our control, we veer away from difficulty and challenge, including real relationships, probing philosophical questions, and much-needed introspection.

Technological innovation is a vital part of our creation mandate to be fruitful and exercise dominion. However, as followers of Jesus in our Monday world, it is important that we are discerning about how subtle and constant technological innovation often comes to us with numbing distractions, better profit margins, and utopian promises. We place our ultimate trust not in technology but in God.

One of the most alluring ways we can be wooed into technological idolatry is artificial intelligence (AI). As artificial intelligence advances, we can let it push God off the thrones of wisdom, creation, morality, and our identity. As a society we may drift toward taking all our questions and problems, big and small, to machine learning and ignore God and his Word. We may befriend artificial agents and give them more of ourselves than we do our incarnational, human relationships. We may try to ease the angst in our soul with AI balm rather than the boundless love of God. We need discernment in using AI.

Clearly, AI is one of the most dynamic technological tools of our time. An AI bot was asked, "What does AI technology mean for humanity?" It responded, "In the annals of human history, there are moments that stand out as turning points, where the fate of humanity hangs in the balance. The discovery of fire, the invention of the wheel, the harnessing of electricity—all of these were moments that transformed human civilization, altering the course of history forever. And now we stand at the brink of another such moment as we face the rise of a coming wave of technology that includes both advanced AI and biotechnology. Never before have we witnessed technologies with such transformative potential, promising to reshape the world in ways that are both awe-inspiring and daunting."[5]

AI brings with it a lot of hope and hype as well as heart-arresting concern. Computers are becoming faster and smarter, inventing tools and technology that we cannot fully foresee or fathom.[6] How AI itself will evolve and continue to change our lives is unknown. Its potential for good and bad outcomes and unintended consequences is up for thoughtful debate. Yet we can be confident that AI is increasingly becoming a part of our everyday lives and our work. In my workplace, I have available on my computer a digital research assistant that makes an entire world of knowledge available to me. AI can also craft emails, write blog posts, and compose journal articles in my vocabulary style and voice. In many workplaces, AI assists in writing policy, in financial management, and in formulating strategy. AI-driven robots are present in our places of work, especially in manufacturing and warehousing. It is making self-driving vehicles possible. Physicians and mental health professionals use AI to assist them in diagnosing a patient and formulating treatments and patient care plans. This technology is ubiquitous in our ever-changing workplaces.

Like any technology, AI brings with it both possibilities and perils. One of the early developers of AI, Mustafa Suleyman, offers his perspective: "I believe this coming wave of technology is bringing human history to a turning point. If containing it is impossible, the consequences for our species are dramatic, potentially dire. Equally, without its fruits we are exposed and precarious."[7] Although Suleyman paints AI as both good and bad, he sees this advancing technology as vital for human flourishing moving forward. He has called for regulatory oversight and containment to mitigate the possibility of grave misuse of AI, such as the evaporation of privacy, deepfake identities, and the destructive potential of its weaponization.

Artificial intelligence will also cause significant workplace disruption. New economic efficiencies as well as new costs will emerge. Almost no job sector will be unaffected. Many jobs will either go away completely or be greatly altered. But though many jobs will be lost or significantly transformed, it is a hopeful possibility that many new less tedious, more creative jobs will be created. Yet it is also possible, because of the sweeping nature of AI and its exponential humanlike capacities, that a more massive economic disruption will take place.[8]

AI brings new possibilities and new challenges. Emotional stress and organizational turmoil can be expected during times of disruptive technological transition. Artificial intelligence also presents ethical challenges involving intellectual property and plagiarism. How does proper human attribution and monetization of human creativity and value take place in an AI world? How might machine learning perpetuate social biases and inequality? How will we build an ethical AI?

Many mental health professionals also express concern about the consequences of AI in further isolating people as a result of reduced embodied connection. As followers of Jesus we will need to be discerning about the ethical use of AI and become advocates for preventing its misuse. We must not attempt to replace God with AI. We must nurture incarnational relationships as a priority.

If there is one thing we can be sure of in our Monday worlds, it is technological change. But we don't have to face those changes alone, nor do we need to fear. What we need to do is wisely embrace change by coming to our risen Savior, who is prepared to help us navigate those changes as his redemptive agents. One of those dynamic changes is remote work.

What about Remote Work?

Technology has made it possible for many to work remotely. How should we think about this change? There are many positive aspects to remote work. It can lead to greater time and cost efficiencies in eliminating commuting, along with greater environmental benefits. For many workers, remote work offers greater flexibility and work-life balance. Many parents with careers who are raising small children find the remote work option much more conducive for their own and their family's well-being. Smaller for-profit and nonprofit organizations can recruit better talent when remote work is offered and relocation is not required.

Remote work also has its downsides. It can be isolating, hindering productivity. The lack of both planned and spontaneous flesh-and-blood interaction with colleagues can be impoverishing on a personal level and can hinder the collaborative creativity that comes with working together in a common workplace. Building and maintaining organizational culture is also a big challenge.

I often hear work leaders bemoan the difficulty of fostering organizational culture and interpersonal comradery when remote work is the norm. The nonprofit Made to Flourish, which I serve, has a blend of on-site and remote employees and takes a more hybrid approach. Our leadership offers a good deal of flexibility to all our employees yet encourages on-site presence as much as possible. For all employees, both on-site and remote, we plan regular gatherings throughout the year for embodied presence, allowing for face-to-face interaction. While we are regularly digitally connected, we know that is not the same as being physically present. As an organization, we now need to be much more intentional about ensuring physical presence than we have in the past, when remote work was the rare exception and relocation was the norm. If most of your work is done remotely, take advantage of the unique opportunities it affords. But also be intentional to compensate for its unintended consequences and potential pitfalls. If done well, remote work can be a place of flourishing.

New Entrepreneurial Opportunities

Rather than seeing technological change as an obstacle, we can view it as an opportunity for entrepreneurial energy and new endeavors. As a young professional, Emily Stewart was feeling disconnected from her college and work friends as her demanding career was starting. Inspired by her faith and the desperate need of her peers, she launched Belong For Me, built on an AI-powered platform she calls "CoExperiences," to connect employees within an organization. The CoExperiences AI engine matches employees based on shared interests. Then it schedules and books curated events based on those interests. This solution saves money for employers, while employees have fun building friendships and confronting the isolation epidemic faced by young workers in a highly digitized workspace.[9]

As a pastor, I often speak with congregants who have lost their job. Job loss can occur for many reasons, one of which is technological efficiency that has reduced a worker's value to a company. As apprentices of Jesus who embrace God's story of work, job loss, though stressful, can be an opportunity to trust God's goodness and provision. Disruptive change could be a new door opening. Trusting in God and peering through the eyes of faith, perhaps now is the time to embrace an energizing entrepreneurial posture of creativity, confidence, and resilience. Both welcome and unwelcome change bring new opportunity.

I find it fascinating that the conclusion of the wisdom book of Proverbs lauds a wise woman: "Give her the reward of her labor, and let her works praise her at the city gates" (Prov. 31:31). In this ancient cultural context, the city gates were the for-profit marketplace where goods were sold. Proverbs closes by highlighting not a king or a priest but an industrious and entrepreneurial businesswoman. This speaks to the good and important contribution that wise entrepreneurs can make in God's kingdom and in our marketplaces today.

In whatever career season you find yourself, if you face a job loss or transition, allow the needed time to pause and evaluate your own gifts and experience. In this liminal space, slow down and become more attentive to the emerging needs around you in both the non-profit and for-profit marketplaces. If you find yourself in a time of unemployment or job transition, perhaps a new entrepreneurial opportunity is awaiting you. Entrepreneurship is not for everyone and comes with risk, but be willing to consider this possibility. Assuming an entrepreneurial posture, look carefully and listen attentively to the needs of others. Take the time to think outside the box. What creative solutions to problems can you explore? What value can you bring to others that has the possibility of being monetized and becoming economically sustainable? What expertise will you need to gain, how much capital will be required, and who can provide mentoring wisdom?[10]

However your workplace is changing, remember that God is always with you. He delights in you and your work. He has made you creative. God has your back and is ahead of you. In a fast-changing world, none of us know what the future holds, but we do know who holds our future. God is in charge and is moving history forward to a good end. Today you can do your work with the anticipation that Jesus will return and set the world right. Perhaps that will be soon. In your Monday world, you are safe and secure in his loving, sovereign, nail-scarred hands.

A Prayer for Change

Amid so much uncertainty and change, Jesus Christ, you are the same yesterday, today, and forever. Guard my heart from fear, grant me discernment, and help me to trust your sovereign hand as new technology develops. Thank you for going before us and being with us. Amen.

Questions for Reflection and Discussion

- What technological change has had the biggest impact on your work recently? In what ways has that been helpful or harmful in your experience?

- Where is technology a gift in your work? Where has it been an idol in your life and work?

- How can we ensure we're not overly trusting technology as we use it, and instead depend on God?

- How has technological innovation cultivated fear or anxiety in your life? Take time to surrender those fears or anxieties to Jesus, knowing that he holds your life more than any technological advancement.

- As a Christian, how can you leverage technology to cultivate compassion, justice, and stewardship in your spheres of influence?

11

Your Monday Mission

Every disciple of Jesus is called to be a minister of the gospel
in his or her workplace. Wherever we are engaged in the efforts of his kingdom, we are acting as ministers administrating
God's goodwill on earth as it is in heaven.

—Dallas Willard[1]

Through the outreach of a parachurch organization, Steve Doerr became a follower of Jesus. As a talented college athlete, Steve excelled
on the soccer field, leading his team to the national championship
game. With offers to become a professional athlete, Steve wrestled
with how his Christian faith should inform his career choice. The
parachurch organization that introduced Steve to Jesus often com-
municated the mindset that only two things were ultimately important: people's souls and God's Word; all the rest was temporal. Steve
concluded that if he wanted to give his life for what really mattered,
he would pursue a calling that was solely devoted to evangelism and
discipleship. Christian parachurch workers, pastors, and missionaries gave their lives to what really mattered.

With a great deal of dissonance in his mind and heart, following college, Steve pursued a career in professional soccer and then in international business. Yet for the decades that followed, even though Steve pursued his relationship with Jesus, was a vital part of a faith community, and shared his faith with colleagues, a cloud of doubt hung over his mind and heart. As a Christian, had he settled for second best? Had his work mattered for eternity? Should he have pursued the pastorate or become a parachurch worker or a missionary to an unreached people group? These thoughts haunted him. As he moved toward retirement, something a conference speaker said caught his attention: "Why settle for being a pastor if God has called you to be a businessman?" He had never heard a Christian leader put it that way before, but something struck a chord.

Following retirement from his global business career, Steve moved to Kansas City and began attending the church community that I have the privilege of serving. It was here for the first time that Steve began to hear God's story of work and see through the cloud of doubt and dissonance surrounding his calling and career. While we were having coffee one morning, Steve looked at me and with eyes twinkling said, "Tom, because I did not pursue being a pastor or missionary, every morning that I woke up, I felt as if I was on God's B-team. But now, grasping God's work story, I realize I have always been on God's A-team. You have no idea how transformational learning God's work story has been for me."

God's A-Team

I interact with many followers of Jesus like Steve who live under a dark cloud, believing that their work is second best, that they somehow are on God's B-team, while others pursuing "spiritual" vocations are on God's A-team. Maybe that has been your experience. Perhaps for a long time you have entered your work world with this mindset hanging over you. In saying this, I am in no way disparaging the important callings of pastors, parachurch workers, or missionaries. These callings matter, and if God calls you to serve him in that way, it is important that you follow his leading. Yet all followers of Jesus who prayerfully seek God's guidance and faithfully serve him are on God's A-team, regardless of where they work.

Remembering Where We Have Been

In chapters 1–5 we explored God's work story. We looked at how he designed work in his original creation. We also explored how work has gone badly awry in humankind's disobedience to God and subsequent fall into sin and brokenness. We then reflected on God's plan to redeem us as workers, our work itself, and our workplaces. We also contemplated the hopeful and heartwarming future of our work in the new heavens and new earth. We took a closer look at Jesus not only as our Lord and Savior but also as a worker who spent the majority of his time on earth laboring with his hands in a Nazareth carpentry shop. This Jesus created the very tree that was cruelly crafted to crucify him as he voluntarily laid down his life as an atonement for our sins. This Jesus who was raised from the dead is with us in our work. As his apprentices, we learn from him how to do our work and how we are to love others in our workplace as fellow image bearers of God.

The biblical story of work is filled with great purpose, joy, and hope. We are wonderfully called and equipped to live into that story in our Monday worlds. Becoming an apprentice of Jesus calls us to whole-life discipleship, and a large part of our lives is our paid and unpaid work. In the workplace, our vocational discipleship and mission come together in transformational, strategic, and joyful ways. You may not think of yourself as a missionary in the traditional sense, but Jesus has sent you on a great mission to your Monday workplace.

In chapters 6–10, we explored how your Monday world is a primary place of worship, meaning, and growth. We also reflected on your workplace as a primary place of loving your neighbor. We examined some of the challenging realities we experience in our workplaces in a fallen world, where for many of us work itself is rapidly changing. As we now wrap up our exploration of God's work story and how we live into it, we are going to see that our work and the workplaces we inhabit are our primary place of influence.

A Primary Place of Influence

What comes to mind when you hear the word "church"? Many people think of that place, even that building, where people regularly attend corporate worship. While our regular attendance and commitment to a local church is vitally important, "church" connotes more than where we gather each week. The church is every one of its members, from the youngest to the oldest, who are called to be apprentices of Jesus, growing in intimacy with him, working with him, and joining him in his kingdom mission in the world.

Following his bodily resurrection and just prior to his ascension to heaven, Jesus left his followers with final instructions regarding their influential mission in the world. In Matthew's Gospel we read, "Then Jesus came to them and said, 'All authority in heaven and on earth has been given to me. Therefore go and make disciples of all nations, baptizing them in the name of the Father and of the Son and of the Holy Spirit, and teaching them to obey everything that I have commanded you. And surely I am with you always, to the very end of the age'" (Matt. 28:18–20 NIV). Jesus's Great Commission reminds us that an essential part of our calling to whole-life discipleship is helping others become disciples of Jesus.

Where does our commission to make disciples take place? It happens everywhere Jesus calls us to go, including our immediate family and proximate neighborhoods. For a large part of our week we are called to go and make disciples in our spheres of paid and unpaid work. Jesus's final words of mission are built on the original creation mandate to work, the Great Commandment calling to love our neighbors, and the invitation to become his yoked apprentice. Jesus's final words for our Monday mission are like theological frosting on the cake of God's work story—the joyful sweetness of seeing others come to faith in Jesus and following him. We need to see the Great Commission through the lens of God's work story. Yet so often we do not think of our Monday workplace as a primary setting of kingdom influence or gospel mission. We can gain greater clarity when we learn from early church history.

Learning from the Past

There's a remarkable parallel between the first-century world and our own. The world Jesus came to was in many ways uniquely positioned for his earliest followers to take the gospel to the ends of the earth. As the apostle Paul writes in Galatians 4:4, "But when the fullness of time had come, God sent forth his Son" (ESV). While Paul's inspired words capture that opportune moment of redemptive history, God had all along carefully arranged the chessboard of all human history.

The first-century Roman world provided just the right conditions for spreading the gospel from a remote and obscure part of the world. The Pax Romana, the peace of Rome, created a sense of stability that allowed the gospel to spread, and the building of remarkable Roman roads facilitated travel. Both the Pax Romana and the Roman road system allowed the gospel and church planting to spread rapidly during the first three centuries AD. In addition, the Greek language became the lingua franca of commerce and intellectual discourse. It is not incidental that the New Testament writers, appealing to a global audience, penned the Bible in Greek.

Church historian Alan Kreider points to the marketplace as a main catalyst for the rapid spread of the gospel and growth of the early church. Ordinary Christians, not clergy, were the key to gospel expansion. Kreider states, "Christians followed their business opportunities." He notes that non-Christians observed the Christian difference in the marketplace, such as the "patient way the Christians operate their businesses." Their vocational discipleship and mission had a profound impact on their culture: "Non-Christians and Christians worked together and lived near each other. They became friends."[2]

We can learn much from first-century followers of Jesus. In a similar way to their moment in redemptive history, our world is an open door of opportunity for followers of Jesus. Like the Pax Romana and the Roman roads, both the internet and the global economy have brought the world together in unprecedented ways. The English language and the US dollar facilitate the global economy. Some of us enter this global world every Monday and are more likely to converse with an English-speaking colleague in India than a neighbor across the street. The twenty-first century is amazingly interconnected, and its missional intersection often occurs in the Monday marketplace. Perhaps this is why Billy Graham pointed to the marketplace as to where he believed the next great movement of God would occur.

As a pastor, I long to share the good news of Jesus with others, and I hope that more and more people will find their way to church to hear the message and be equipped to follow him. Yet I know the vast majority of people in our community, our city, and our nation will not enter the door of our church, or any church for that matter. But I also know God has sent his followers into every nook and cranny of society through their various callings, followers of Jesus like you. You are on mission as his witness to all those he has positioned near you in the places where you work.

Most of us live and work in a context where certain assumptions make God's reality and his revelation seem implausible and incoherent. As a result, the Christian faith we cherish is often dismissed and rejected out of hand. In many ways our times are similar to the early centuries of the church, yet that was a time of amazing gospel proclamation, expansion, and transformation. How was that possible? Certainly, it was in part because of the power of the gospel itself and the supernatural empowering of the Holy Spirit. But it is also true that the early followers of Jesus witnessed for him as they lived out the gospel in their ordinary day-to-day lives, a great deal of which were spent in their particular workplace.

Other people often need to see the good news of the gospel lived out by us before it is truly heard from us. Though we are called to verbally profess our faith, we are also called to practice it. Yes, we witness by our words, but we also witness by our work. The words we speak must be validated by our Christlike witness. Our virtuous lives, our love for others, and our excellent work all contribute toward persuading others around us of the goodness, beauty, and truth of our faith. The excellence of our work often gives us the credibility with our coworkers to speak of the excellence of our Lord Jesus and to share the good news of the gospel. Jesus points out that our good work makes us salt and light in the world and compels those who are not yet his followers to be drawn to God the Father and his kingdom (Matt. 5:14–16).

The sheer amount of time you work each week means you witness much more by your work than you do by your words. God designed it that way and has specifically placed us in our Monday world to join him on his redemptive rescue mission. Let's press more into what that means for you in your Monday mission.

Becoming a More Excellent Worker

The writer of Ecclesiastes encourages us to pursue excellence in our work: "Whatever your hand finds to do, do it with all your might" (Eccles. 9:10 NIV). As an apprentice of Jesus, continuing to grow in your vocational competence is an important aspect of whole-life discipleship. Keep Dorothy Sayers's insightful words close to your heart as you enter your Monday workplace: "The only Christian work is good work well done."[3] How "Christian" is your work these days? Are you known by the various stakeholders, clients, patients, or customers you serve as a virtuous, loving person who always does great work? Are you continuing to stay curious about your work, maintaining a teachable attitude, participating in webinars, or continuing educational opportunities? Are you learning new technologies in your trade and gaining new skills and competencies?

I have had the joy of knowing Mike O'Connell for over thirty years. A former Marine, Mike is a no-nonsense guy who can do anything with his hands. Mike is a continual learner in his craft, always seeking ways to enhance his skills. Seeing the need for greater comfort and energy conservation in buildings, Mike founded a local insulation business that assists thousands of homeowners and businesses with their insulation needs and energy-saving opportunities. Mike's small business has flourished with a triple bottom line in mind—serving people well, making a consistent profit, and caring for the planet. Embracing God's story of work, Mike is on mission, seeing the high quality of his Monday work as a primary way he worships God and loves his neighbors.

Travel can be very taxing, especially when it's for work. Over the years, I have spent considerable time in airports. Hanging out in a sea of strangers can be exhausting and disorienting. Ordering a cup of coffee or grabbing a breakfast burrito can make a big difference to the start of my day in meeting not only the cries of a hungry stomach but also the longings of a hungry soul. My experience with those who make my airport coffee is a regular reminder of how much our work matters in accomplishing tasks and in responding and relating to other image bearers of God. When a barista hands me my coffee in a bustling airport, a smile warms my soul. Christian work is not only the quality of work we do but also the loving way we treat others. How we relate in serving others or treating those who serve us is an indicator of how we are living into God's story of work.

The work we are called to do is a place to serve others well and a primary context for forging meaningful friendships. In great measure the quality of our lives is seen in the quality of our relationships. Are we nurturing friendships in our work? When we make relationships a top priority, we wisely and lovingly begin with a posture of respect and reverence for our fellow image bearers. C. S. Lewis writes, "There are no ordinary people. You have never talked to a mere mortal. Nations, cultures, arts, civilizations—these are mortal, and their life is to ours as the life of a gnat. But it is immortals whom we joke with, work with, marry, snub and exploit—immortal horrors or everlasting splendors. Next to the Blessed Sacrament itself, your neighbor is the holiest object presented to your senses."[4] What a difference it would make if we saw each person we encountered in our workplace through such a gracious and illuminating lens. At our most basic level, each one of us needs to feel seen, respected, valued, and understood by others.

Take the initiative to get to know others in your world of work. Embrace an explorer's posture of curiosity. Ask others questions that allow them to tell their stories. David Brooks reminds us of the importance of the art of conversation: "A good conversationalist is a master of fostering a two-way exchange. A good conversationalist is capable of leading people on a mutual expedition toward understanding."[5] Even a cursory glance at the New Testament reveals Jesus was not only a brilliant teacher but also a master conversationalist.[6] Growing in emotional intelligence and making relationships a top priority in your workplace allows you to love others well and reflects our Lord and Savior.

Common Grace for the Common Good

God's work story reminds us that all human beings are created in the image of God and have intrinsic value and inherent dignity. In his most famous sermon, Jesus teaches, "For he causes his sun to rise on the evil and the good, and sends rain on the righteous and the unrighteous" (Matt. 5:45). Jesus points his listeners to the loving Father, who cares for the needs of all his image bearers—even those who reject him and his good ways. Theologians often refer to Jesus's teaching here as common grace.

As God's image bearers, we are to reflect his common grace to others, and in many ways this love for our neighbor is directed toward people who may not be very neighborly. Common grace is not the same as saving grace, which only God can initiate toward those who have not yet embraced Jesus as their personal Lord and Savior. Yet I find that often the common grace we extend to others becomes the fertile soil for saving grace to emerge in their hearts and minds. In his mysterious sovereignty, God has designed common grace to express his unfathomable love as a wooing conduit for saving grace to find its way home to the longing human heart. Your Monday workplace is an extraordinary opportunity to foster common grace for the common good. Consider with me the stories of a few workers who embody this pursuit of the common good especially well.

Tracy Foster, along with two other moms, was increasingly concerned about how much screen time their elementary-age children were spending on phones, laptop computers, and televisions. As they began to research this problem, they realized that a whole generation of parents is struggling with this issue. With the help of a handful of wise advisers, Tracy cofounded Screen Sanity, an international nonprofit that equips parents to help their kids navigate an increasingly digital world.[7] As a follower of Jesus, Tracy has embraced God's work story, which has compelled her to address a growing need. She has embraced her Monday mission with common grace and the common good in mind.

Rod Brenneman is a former CEO with extensive banking experience and influential business contacts in Kansas City. He began to see a glaring injustice perpetrated on the most economically vulnerable members of the city by the oppressive payday loan industry. Rod prayed and started dreaming of how he could be an agent of redemption and foster the common good of the city. He took the initiative by bringing business leaders together and creating a new path forward where banks could get community credits, individuals from low-income communities could obtain liquidity loans at low interest rates, and nonprofit organizations could provide the care and financial counseling needed to put many of the most vulnerable on a more sustainable path. The most economically vulnerable now have another option for their liquidity needs and are not forced to take out exorbitant high-interest loans from payday lenders. In retirement, Rod is embracing his Monday mission, fostering the common good and heeding the prophet Micah's words, "What does the LORD require of you but to do justice, and to love kindness, and to walk humbly with your God?" (Mic. 6:8 ESV).

Robin John's life and Monday work world are being shaped by God's story of work. So much so that he and his friend Finny Kuruvilla launched a values-based asset management firm. Eventide now manages billions of dollars by investing with a values-based lens framed from a biblical worldview. Robin, the CEO of Eventide, puts it this way: "Together, we strive to honor God and serve our clients by investing in companies that create compelling value for the global common good. Our dream isn't just to have a successful company, but to help every Christian and values-based investor to invest in ways that align both with their financial goals and their core beliefs about what is good, true, and beautiful. . . . But what I am most joyful about is that we have been able to build a very diverse team of both Christians and non-Christians who all share our passion for what we call 'investing that makes the world rejoice.'"[8] When spending time with Robin, who is an apprentice of Jesus, I continually hear his heart cry of loving our neighbor well through the investment decisions we make. Eventide is part of a faith-driven investing and entrepreneurial movement helping followers of Jesus live more fully into God's story of work as it relates to impact investing and expanding philanthropic capacity.[9] Robin has been transformed by God's story of work and is embracing his Monday mission.

As an experienced entrepreneur, Dave Blanchard longed for entrepreneurship to be framed through the lens of the biblical story, so he cofounded Praxis Labs. His heart was to equip and encourage a new generation of entrepreneurs who would put their faith into action in the global marketplace. Dave and his gifted and devoted team are creating a venture-building ecosystem that fosters redemptive entrepreneurship, which they define as follows: "The

189

redemptive way is creative restoration through sacrifice—to bless others, renew culture, and give of ourselves. Redemptive actors pursue an 'I sacrifice, we win' approach with the agency and resources available to them. The motivating force behind the Redemptive way is fundamentally other-centered: to love and serve."[10] Praxis Labs encourages entrepreneurs to move from an exploitative mindset to an ethical mindset and finally to a redemptive mindset. A redemptive mindset is about embracing a Monday mission of entrepreneurs who love their neighbors well in and through their work and serve the common good. Dave and his team help entrepreneurs become agents of flourishing who display pockets of greatness, goodness, truth, and beauty in the marketplace.

Your Work Matters

Your work calling may not involve entrepreneurial start-ups aimed at solving a large societal problem. Dan Ott's work calling is as a wastewater engineer. His work is not often visible or flashy. But his good work helps to design and ensure safe and sanitary conditions for an entire community. In the maturation season of his career, Dan now embraces the stewardship of generativity by mentoring younger engineers. God's A-team often works quietly in obscure spaces to love their neighbors and promote the common good.

Whatever season of work you are in, whether called to be a teacher, lab technician, food service or retail worker, software developer, landscaper, nurse, or stay-at-home parent, you are a vital part of God's amazing story of work. Throughout this book, we have looked through the window of God's story and can now see ourselves and our work fitting beautifully into his story.

Whatever work God has called you to will be in a broken world and will include a mixture of the enjoyable, the exhausting, and the exasperating. The people you encounter will be a mixture of the good, the wise, the foolish, and, yes, even sometimes evil. Yet as an apprentice of Jesus, no matter where God has called you in your

Monday world, you are on his A-team. God has called you to be on mission with him. Jesus would be perfectly at home in your job, and undertaking your work with him is your greatest opportunity.

The work you are doing really matters. If you are not yet a part of a local church community, let me encourage you to find a church family that will encourage your spiritual formation and equip you as a disciple of Jesus in your Monday workplace.[11] As part of a vibrant local church, you can remain buoyant and hopeful in the work God calls you to do, no matter what season you are in or how much you may like it or dislike it.

Peter Berger, one of the premier sociologists of our time, once visited our church. A group of young pastors who were part of our clergy residency program gathered to glean his wisdom and asked whether he considered himself a Christian. Berger, with his towering intellect, paused and said, "Yes, I do. Something happened on Easter morning two thousand years ago the world has not got over and neither have I."[12] Like Berger, we look into an empty tomb in amazement and have hope that death is not the final word. We hope not only for the eternal life our hearts long for but also for the enduring meaning of our daily work, that somehow our work really matters.

In his most expansive writing on the bodily resurrection of Jesus, the apostle Paul concludes his thoughts by peering through the lens of God's work story: "Therefore, my beloved brothers and sisters, be firm, immovable, always excelling in the work of the Lord, knowing that your labor is not in vain in the Lord" (1 Cor. 15:58 NASB). As an apprentice to our risen and ever-present Savior, any work you do for his glory and with love for your neighbor is never in vain. Yes, your Monday work really matters. You are on God's A-team.

A Prayer of Hope

May the God of hope fill you with all joy and peace as you trust in him, so that you may overflow with hope by the power of the Holy Spirit. (Rom. 15:13 NIV)

Questions for Reflection and Discussion

- What unique opportunities do you have to demonstrate faithfulness in your vocation?
- How does the opportunity to be part of God's mission change the way you think about your job?
- How will you exercise your role as a member of God's A-team today?
- What is one practical takeaway from this chapter you want to implement in your life?

Acknowledgments

It has been often said that teamwork makes the dream work. Nothing could be truer in describing the remarkably talented dream team who made this writing project a reality. My pastoral colleague Johnny Daigle has expended unbounding energy, contagious enthusiasm, and hard work bringing his many insights to the manuscript. Steve Harvey, who serves as my executive assistant, has covered countless details in managing my calendar and has guided this project to its completion on time. Steve is not only very capable managing a myriad of details but is also a wise friend. My wife, Liz, has guided calendar decisions as well and has been a constant encouragement, providing wise input for the entire manuscript. Her fingerprints grace every page. A special thanks to my friend Demi Lloyd, who generously provided a quiet and beautiful place to write a good chunk of the manuscript and who lives into this message every day of her workweek.

I want to thank my literary agent, Tom Dean, who has been a source of encouragement, expertise, and wisdom. My heartfelt gratitude to our editorial director, Katelyn Beaty, who has strongly believed in the great importance and potential impact of this book. Katelyn, it has been really great to work with you. I also want to thank the Brazos team—Jim Kinney, Jeremy Wells, Erin Smith, Kara Day, Janelle Mahlmann, Paula Gibson, Eric Salo, Adam Lorenz, and Julie Tinklenberg—for their warmth and professional expertise.

Ben Beasley, Brad Calhoun, Gabe Coyle, Kelly Daigle, Tim Daigle, Nikki Dieker, Bill Gorman, Liz Nelson, Susie Rowan, and Matt Rusten served as early manuscript readers and have offered helpful insight that made the book better. Thanks for your willingness to work so enthusiastically in a short window. A warm word of appreciation to my friend Bill Hendricks, who serves as my executive coach and has a passionate commitment to the Faith, Work, and Economics movement.

I have the joy of working with an amazingly gifted and committed team at Made to Flourish. I especially want to thank Matt Rusten, Kevin Harlan, Eric Jimenez, and Aaron Hanbury, who have been simply magical in their many contributions and insights. I could not have done this project without the strongest encouragement from the Made to Flourish board. A special thanks to the Kern Family Foundation, Jim Rahn, Kyle Bode, and Marcia Peterson, who for many years believed in and encouraged my thought leadership in the broader Faith, Work, and Economics movement. Thanks for being such a strong tailwind in a mission that truly matters. I also want to thank the board, staff, and congregation of Christ Community Church for cheering on the vital work of vocational discipleship and mission, connecting Sunday to Monday.

All praise and honor goes to my Lord and Savior, Jesus, whose brilliant life, sacrificial death, and glorious resurrection daily breathes hope into my heart, soul, mind, and body. For several decades now, I have had the joy of being Jesus's yoked apprentice. Father, may your kingdom come, your will be done on earth as it is in heaven. Soli Deo Gloria.

Notes

Chapter 1 Why Work?

1. Thomas Merton, *No Man Is an Island* (New York: Harcourt Brace, 1955), quoted in Placher, *Callings*, 426.

2. Sinek, *Start with Why*, 39 (formatting slightly modified).

3. Dallas Willard, "Dallas Willard—Transforming the Mind 1: Spiritual Formation and the Thought Life," YouTube, 22:18, posted by Conversatio Divina, May 6, 2021, https://youtu.be/wendLvrTnfs.

4. Thanks to Bill Gorman for this insight.

5. At the outset of exploring God's story of work, it is important to grasp a biblical definition of work and not a prevailing cultural definition.

6. Heschel, *Sabbath*, 36.

7. Gideon Strauss, "Making It New: Andy Crouch Proposes a Different Way for Christians to Engage Culture," *Books & Culture* (September/October 2008), https://www.booksandculture.com/articles/2008/sepoct/2.10.html.

8. God's good creation design does not require marriage. Many people are single a good part of their lives, and some are called to singleness all their lives. Singleness should not be seen in the context of the tragedy of Genesis 3 but in the beautiful mystery of Genesis 1–2. Jesus was single all his life. The apostle Paul affirms the calling of singleness in his first letter to the Corinthians.

9. *Avodah* is used to describe the backbreaking work of God's covenant people making bricks in Egypt as well as the artisans building the temple and the fine craftsmanship of linen workers. *Avodah* also appears in the context of Solomon dedicating the temple. Solomon employs this word as he instructs the priests and Levites regarding their service in leading corporate worship and praise of the one true God. Whether it is making bricks, crafting fine linen, or leading others in corporate praise and worship, the Old Testament writers present a seamless understanding of work and worship. Though there are distinct nuances to *avodah*, a common thread of meaning emerges where work, worship, and service are inextricably linked and intricately connected.

10. Heschel, *Sabbath*, 37.

Chapter 2 Work's Great Tragedy

1. Volf, *Work in the Spirit*, 167.

2. Jelly Roll, "Save Me," *Self Medicated*, BBR Music Group, 2020.

3. At the end of Genesis 3, God's job description for humans to work does not cease. It continues, but work itself and the workplaces humans will inhabit will dramatically change.

4. Immediately following Adam and Eve's sin against God and against each other, they fall into what Dallas Willard defines as the two forms of lovelessness: assault and withdrawal. Willard writes, "The exact nature of the poison of sin in our social dimension is fairly easy to describe, though extremely hard to deal with. It has two forms. They are so closely related that they really are two forms of the same thing: of lovelessness, lack of proper regard and care for others. These two forms are *assault* or attack and *withdrawal* or 'distancing.'" He describes assault this way: "We assault others when we act against what is good for them, even with their consent." He explains withdrawal this way: "We withdraw from someone when we regard their well-being and goodness as matters of indifference to us or perhaps go so far as to despise them. We 'don't care.'" See Willard, *Renovation of the Heart*, 181–82.

5. Dallas Willard, "Divine Conspiracy 1—Jesus and Culture," YouTube, 1:13:25, posted by Dallas Willard Ministries, June 28, 2020, https://www.youtube.com /watch?v=pXEuMxLzmWQ.

6. Collins, *Good to Great*, 85.

7. Larry Kim, "7 Taylor Swift Quotes That Will Make You Work Your Ass Off," *Inc.*, September 30, 2015, https://www.inc.com/larry-kim/these-7-quotes-from -taylor-swift-will-make-you-work-your-ass-off.html.

8. Thornton, *Devotional Prayers*, 19.

Chapter 3 Work's Gospel Transformation

1. Dorothy Sayers, "Vocation in Work," in *A Christian Basis for the Post-War World*, ed. A. E. Baker (New York: Morehouse-Gorham, 1942), quoted in Placher, *Callings*, 406.

2. God says to the serpent, "I will put hostility between you and the woman, and between your offspring and her offspring. He will strike your head, and you will strike his heel" (Gen. 3:15).

3. Keller, *Every Good Endeavor*, 163.

4. John describes it this way: "In the beginning was the Word," and "The Word became flesh" (1:1, 14).

5. Keller, *Every Good Endeavor*, 73.

6. Keller, *Prodigal God*, 34.

7. See Charles, *Secular Vocation*, 59. He points out that this estimate comes from Chris Armstrong. A similar estimate comes from a 2017 survey by researchers in London who concluded the average person in the West, based on a seventy-six-year lifespan and assuming fifty years of paid employment, spends 92,210 hours working.

8. Hunter, *To Change the World*, 247.

9. Steven Garber is professor of marketplace theology and director of the program in leadership, theology, and society at Regent College, Vancouver, BC. For more information, visit https://www.ivpress.com/steven-garber.

10. For more information, see demdaco.com.

Chapter 4 Work's Grand Future

1. Wright, *Surprised by Hope*, 259.
2. The massive tornado struck the town of Greensburg on May 4, 2007.
3. Wright, *Surprised by Hope*, 122.
4. Marshall, *Heaven Is Not My Home*, 30–33.
5. Maltbie Davenport Babcock, "This Is My Father's World," 1901, public domain.
6. Lewis, *Miracles*, 244, 253.
7. Willard, *Divine Conspiracy*, 435.
8. Marshall, *Heaven Is Not My Home*, 11.
9. Keller, *Prodigal God*, 103.
10. Rudyard Kipling, "L'Envoi," in *The Seven Seas* (London: Methuen, 1896), available at https://en.wikisource.org/wiki/The_Seven_Seas/L%27Envoi.

Chapter 5 Jesus the Carpenter

1. Jensen and Payne, *Beginnings*, 15.
2. Willard, *Divine Conspiracy*, 14.
3. Dyer, *From the Garden to the City*, chap. 9.
4. Martin Luther King Jr., "Facing the Challenge of a New Age," in *A Testament of Hope: The Essential Writings and Speeches of Martin Luther King, Jr.* (New York: HarperCollins, 1986), 139, quoted in Miller, *God at Work*, 19.
5. Luther, quoted in Wingren, *Luther on Vocation*, 10.
6. Paul reminds them that the gospel had not come to them in word only but "also in power and in the Holy Spirit and with full conviction" (1 Thess. 1:5 ESV). The authenticity of their conversion to Christ was evident in that they "turned to God from idols to serve the living and true God, and to wait for his Son from heaven, whom he raised from the dead, Jesus who delivers us from the wrath to come" (1 Thess. 1:9–10 ESV).
7. Sherman, *Kingdom Calling*, 67.
8. Miller, *God at Work*, 10.
9. Sayers, "Why Work?," 195.

Chapter 6 Thank God It's Monday

1. Beckett, *Loving Monday*, 176.
2. In his work *A Secular Age*, Charles Taylor discusses what he calls "the imminent frame" as a secularized disenchanted workplace.
3. Author's personal conversation with Bob Kern.
4. Frankl, *Man's Search for Meaning*, chap. 2. See also Harold Kushner, foreword to Frankl, *Man's Search for Meaning*.
5. Charles, *Wisdom and Work*, 80. For further reading and reflection, see J. Daryl Charles's excellent book *Our Secular Vocation: Rethinking the Church's Calling to the Marketplace*.
6. Every time we walk through a doorway or open our computer can remind us of God's presence. As we do our work, we can do it under his authority and for his good purposes. In so doing, we can experience God working with us.
7. Daniels and Vandewarker, *Working in the Presence of God*, 40–41.

8. Crawford, *Shop Class as Soulcraft*, 126.
9. Volf, *Work in the Spirit*, 98.
10. Wingreen, *Luther on Vocation*, 33.
11. Willard, *Divine Conspiracy*, 348–49.

Chapter 7 Neighborly Love

1. Luther, quoted in Wingren, *Luther on Vocation*, 10.
2. Klaus Issler, "Examining Jesus' Inclusion of Work Roles in His Parables," Institute for Faith, Work and Economics, accessed February 10, 2017, http://tifwe .org/wp-content/uploads/2014/04/Jesus-and-the-Parables1.pdf, p. 4.
3. See also parallel gospel texts where the Great Commandment is highlighted (Matt. 22:34–40; Mark 12:28–34).
4. The man refers to both Leviticus 19:18 and Deuteronomy 6:5 in his formulation of the Great Commandment.
5. Luke employs this Greek word *splagchnon* only three times in his Gospel (7:13; 10:33; 15:20). Each time *splagchnon* is used it is in the context of intense feelings of pity or sympathy evoked by dire economic need of another person. The apostle John also uses this word in 1 John 3:17, describing negatively the absence of brotherly love, of someone who sees a brother in economic need and "closes his heart against him" (ESV).
6. Bailey, *Jesus through Middle Eastern Eyes*, 290.
7. Claar and Klay, *Economics in Christian Perspective*, 166.
8. Sowell, *Basic Economics*, 213.
9. Martin Luther, *Kirchenpostille* (1522), in *D. Martin Luthers Werke*, 65 vols., Weimarer Ausgabe (Weimar: Böhlau, 1883–1993), vol. 10/1, subpart 1, pp. 491–92, quoted in Wingren, *Luther on Vocation*, 10.
10. Willard and Black, *Divine Conspiracy Continued*, 197.
11. Corbett and Fikkert, *When Helping Hurts*, 56.
12. For further discussion of a biblical framework for economic flourishing, see Nelson, *Economics of Neighborly Love*.
13. Grudem and Asmus, *Poverty of Nations*, 207.
14. Email message to author, September 16, 2015.
15. Collins, *Good to Great*.

Chapter 8 Avoiding Burnout

1. Kapic, *You're Only Human*, 223.
2. For more information, see Lisa Bannon, "When AI Overrules the Nurses Caring for You," *Wall Street Journal*, June 15, 2023, https://www.wsj.com/articles /ai-medical-diagnosis-nurses-f881b0fe.
3. For more information on pastoral burnout, see "Excerpt: A Rapid Decline in Pastoral Security," Barna, March 15, 2023, https://www.barna.com/research/pastoral -security-confidence.
4. The cultural water we swim in is changing in fundamental ways. For greater exploration and understanding of how people in our context grasp the idea of faith, see Hunter, *To Change the World*. Our increasingly secular social imaginary is compellingly presented in Taylor, *Secular Age*. In *The Rise and Triumph of the Modern Self*, Carl R. Trueman makes a strong argument that our sense of self-identity and formation

has radically changed. In addition, our Christian faith is increasingly marginalized, ridiculed, and even vigorously opposed. George Yancey's research focuses on the growing hostility toward Christians and the Christian faith in the media, marketplace, and education. Yancey's conclusion regarding anti-Christian bias and hostility, based on empirical evidence, is compelling and sobering. For more information on George Yancey, visit https://sociology.artsandsciences.baylor.edu/person/george-yancey.

5. Spring 2023 Renovaré newsletter.

6. Patrick Lencioni and his team at the Table Group have developed a helpful tool called Working Genius that can help avoid burnout due to poor job fit. Other tools I recommend are the Clifton StrengthsFinder, DISC assessment, and Myers-Briggs Type Indicator.

7. I would encourage you to read the remarkable and inspiring story of Elijah in 1 Kings 19:1–18. As you read the story, reflect on it through the lens of burnout. What observations do you make about Elijah's burnout? What contributed to it? What made it possible for Elijah to move from the black hole of burnout to a hopeful buoyancy in his work?

8. Bill Gaultiere, "A Simple Solution to Stress from Dallas Willard," Soul Shepherding, accessed August 21, 2024, https://www.soulshepherding.org/a-simple-solution-to-stress-from-dallas-willard.

9. "Very early in the morning, while it was still dark, he got up, went out, and made his way to a deserted place; and there he was praying" (Mark 1:35).

10. For more context of Jesus's words, see Mark 6:30–32.

11. Cited in Comer, *Ruthless Elimination of Hurry*, 18–19.

12. For an insightful reflection, see Kapic, *You're Only Human*.

13. "And on the seventh day God finished his work that he had done, and he rested on the seventh day from all his work that he had done. So God blessed the seventh day and made it holy, because on it God rested from all his work that he had done in creation" (Gen. 2:2–3 ESV).

14. "Remember the Sabbath day, to keep it holy: You are to labor six days and do all your work, but the seventh day is a Sabbath to the LORD your God. You must not do any work—you, your son or daughter, your male or female servant, your livestock, or the resident alien who is within your city gates. For the LORD made the heavens and the earth, the sea, and everything in them in six days; then he rested on the seventh day. Therefore the LORD blessed the Sabbath day and declared it holy" (Exod. 20:8–11).

15. Heschel, *Sabbath*, 24.

16. Heschel, *Sabbath*, 19.

17. Alabaster Creative, *Towards Rest*, 80.

18. Curt Thompson, interview with Tish Harrison Warren, "What if Burnout Is Less about Work and More about Isolation?," *New York Times*, October 9, 2022, https://www.nytimes.com/2022/10/09/opinion/burnout-friends-isolation.html.

19. Jason Shen, "The No. 1 Habit All Highly Resilient People Have, according to a Career Expert," CNBC, March 5, 2024, https://www.cnbc.com/2024/03/05/the-no-1-habit-all-highly-resilience-people-have-according-to-a-career-expert.html.

20. To learn more about Dan Siegel and Mindsight Institute, see https://mindsightinstitute.com.

21. For more information on the benefits of involvement in a local faith community, see Derek Thompson, "The True Cost of the Churchgoing Bust," *The Atlantic*, April 3, 2024, https://www.theatlantic.com/ideas/archive/2024/04/america-religion-decline-non-affiliated/677951/.

22. Lewis, *Letters to Malcolm*, 93.

23. Lewis, *Weight of Glory*, 61.

Chapter 9 The Changing of Seasons of Work

1. Zunker, *Career, Work, and Mental Health*, 12.

2. Zunker, *Career, Work, and Mental Health*, 86.

3. Zunker, *Career, Work, and Mental Health*, 55. Zunker expands on the various theories: "The key characteristic of the trait-oriented approach is the assumption that individuals have unique patterns of ability and traits that can be objectively measured and correlated with the requirements of various types of jobs. In the social learning and cognitive approach, social conditioning, social position, and life events are thought to significantly influence career choice. Developmental approaches stress that individuals make changes during developmental stages and adapt to changing life roles: Individual development is unique, multifaceted, and multidimensional. One's career development in the person-in-environment perspective is thought to be influenced and constructed within several environmental systems, such as family, church, or synagogue, neighborhood, school, neighbors, friends, workplace, and the culture and customs of the larger environment" (55).

4. Haanen, *Uncommon Guide to Retirement*, 69.

5. Placher, *Callings*, 3.

6. Dik, *Redeeming Work*, 36. I highly recommend Bryan's work, especially for those in the early formative stage of their career. *Redeeming Work* is outstanding for providing research-based evidence and a rich, integral biblical theology, yet it is very practical in its applications and guidance.

7. Pss. 37:18; 139:13–14; Jer. 29:11; Luke 12:7.

8. Hendricks, *Person Called You*, 28.

9. Of all the career-discerning instruments I have utilized, the SIMA approach has been the most insightful and helpful. For more information about the SIMA narrative approach, see https://www.simapartners.com/our-advantage-.

10. Hendricks, *Person Called You*, 130.

11. Buechner, *Wishful Thinking*, 95.

12. Career psychologist Bryan Dik makes the case for the importance of being informed about the many emerging career possibilities. He writes, "One source of information available online is the Occupational Information Network (O*NET), a database maintained by the US Department of Labor. The O*NET is searchable and offers extensive and detailed information about roughly a thousand different occupations. It is the most extensive database of occupational information available in the world and it is free to use at www.onetonline.org." Dik, *Redeeming Work*, 62.

13. For more information on Maslow's hierarchy of learning, see Noel Burch, "Four Stages of Learning," KnowledgeX, April 2021, https://theknowledgex.com/infopedia/four-stages-of-learning.

14. Haanen, *Uncommon Guide to Retirement*, 24.

15. Haanen, *Uncommon Guide to Retirement*, 10.

16. See Jesus's parable of the talents in Matt. 25.

17. Three excellent retirement books I would highly recommend are Haanen, *Uncommon Guide to Retirement*; Bruinsma, *Retirement Reformation*; and Stevens, *Aging Matters*.

18. Stevens, *Aging Matters*, 15.

19. David Brooks is known for his brilliant cultural analysis, but now in the latter stage of his career, he models the high priority of growing in emotional intelligence and relational depth. Regardless of the stage of our career, I would highly recommend his book *How to Know a Person*. We are never too young or old to better learn how to know others and be known.

20. Stevens, *Aging Matters*, 52.

Chapter 10 The Changing World of Work

1. Dyer, *From the Garden to the City*, chap. 1.

2. Learn more about the Grohmann Museum at https://www.msoe.edu/groh mann-museum.

3. Dyer, *From the Garden to the City*, chap. 1.

4. Dyer, *From the Garden to the City*, chap. 1.

5. Suleyman, *Coming Wave*, 3–4.

6. Some definitional clarification can be helpful. Artificial narrow intelligence (ANI) describes machines that are really good at one thing. Artificial general intelligence (AGI) describes machines that are as good as humans on many fronts. Artificial super intelligence (ASI) describes the possibility of machines becoming better than humans at virtually everything.

7. Suleyman, *Coming Wave*, 7.

8. Mustafa Suleyman evaluates AI's job disruption this way: "On job loss and unemployment—technological unemployment, tech-related displacement—in the past technological changes produced new jobs. But what if new job displacement systems scale the ladder of human cognitive ability itself, leaving nowhere new for labor to turn? If the coming wave really is as general and wide-ranging as it appears, how will humans compete? What if a large majority of white-collar tasks can be performed more efficiently by AI?" Suleyman, *Coming Wave*, 178.

9. For more information on Belong for Me, see https://belongforme.com/our -story.

10. For additional entrepreneurial resources from the Kauffman Foundation and Praxis Labs, see https://www.kauffman.org and https://www.praxislabs .org.

Chapter 11 Your Monday Mission

1. Willard and Black, *Divine Conspiracy Continued*, 214.

2. Kreider, *Patient Ferment of the Early Church*, 144, 149.

3. Sayers, "Why Work?," in Schwehn and Bass, *Leading Lives That Matter*, 195.

4. Lewis, *Weight of Glory*, 46.

5. Brooks, *How to Know a Person*, 72.

6. See, for example, Jesus's masterful conversation with a Samaritan woman in John 4.

7. "Our nonprofit helps families and communities pursue digital health in order to reduce loneliness, depression, anxiety and suicide in a socially isolated society. The need for our programs and resources has only grown in a post-pandemic world, with screens and devices seeping into every corner of our children's lives. Our broader resources and tools are designed to support families on every leg of their digital parenting journey—helping them to quickly navigate to the issue that is most pressing for their own family. Our goal is to build trust with families so when they hit a new technology milestone, they know exactly where to turn." "About," Screen Sanity, accessed July 20, 2024, https://screensanity.org.

8. To learn more about Eventide Investments, visit https://www.eventideinvestments.com/resources/founding.

9. To learn more about Faith Driven Investor, visit https://www.faithdriveninvestor.org. For more information about Faith Driven Entrepreneur, visit https://www.faithdrivenentrepreneur.org.

10. To learn more about Praxis Labs and its mission, visit https://www.praxislabs.org/redemptive-entrepreneurship.

11. I recommend being committed to a local church that emphasizes vocational discipleship and mission. Vocationally informed discipleship is when a church uses its knowledge of the vocational makeup of its congregation to intentionally shape formation pathways and tools in order to equip them to faithfully follow Christ in their everyday work. Vocationally informed mission is when a church utilizes the skills and occupational competencies of its congregation to inform and shape initiatives that help its community flourish. For more information, I invite you to learn more about Made to Flourish (https://www.madetoflourish.org) and to check out *Common Good* magazine (https://commongoodmag.com).

12. I personally heard these words in a meeting with Christ Community Church residents while Berger was in Kansas City.

Bibliography

Alabaster Creative. *Towards Rest: Discovering the Qualities of Rest for Our Lives of Faith.* Pico Rivera, CA: Alabaster Creative, 2021.

Ambrose, Stephen. *Nothing Like It in the World: The Men Who Built the Transcontinental Railroad.* New York: Simon & Schuster, 2000.

Bailey, Kenneth. *Jesus through Middle Eastern Eyes: Cultural Studies in the Gospels.* Downers Grove, IL: IVP Academic, 2008.

Barnes, Kenneth J. *Redeeming Capitalism.* Grand Rapids: Eerdmans, 2018.

Beckett, John D. *Loving Monday: Succeeding in Business without Selling Your Soul.* Downers Grove, IL: IVP Books, 2006.

Bonhoeffer, Dietrich. *The Cost of Discipleship.* New York: Macmillan, 1963.

Brooks, David. *How to Know a Person: The Art of Seeing Others Deeply and Being Seen Deeply.* New York: Random House, 2023.

Bruinsma, Bruce. *The Retirement Reformation: Finding Freedom with Faith . . . A Better Way to Experience the Final (and Best) Decades of Your Life.* Bloomington, IN: Westbow, 2019.

Budziszewski, J. *Evangelicals in the Public Square.* Grand Rapids: Baker Academic, 2006.

Buechner, Frederick. *Wishful Thinking: A Theological ABC.* New York: Harper & Row, 1973.

Busenitz, Lowell. *Soul Work: Finding God in Your Entrepreneurial Pursuits.* Peabody, MA: Hendrickson, 2023.

Carson, Don. *Scandalous: The Cross and Resurrection of Jesus*. Wheaton: Crossway, 2010.

Charles, J. Daryl. *A Secular Vocation: Rethinking the Church's Calling to the Marketplace*. Nashville: B&H Academic, 2023.

———. *Wisdom and Work: Theological Reflections on Human Labor from Ecclesiastes*. Eugene, OR: Wipf & Stock, 2021.

Claar, Victor V., and Robin J. Klay. *Economics in Christian Perspective: Theory, Policy, and Life Choices*. Downers Grove, IL: IVP Academic, 2007.

Collins, Jim. *Good to Great: Why Some Companies Make the Leap and Others Don't*. New York: HarperCollins, 2001.

Comer, John Mark. *The Ruthless Elimination of Hurry*. Colorado Springs: WaterBrook, 2019.

Corbett, Steve, and Brian Fikkert. *When Helping Hurts: How to Alleviate Poverty without Hurting the Poor and Yourself*. Chicago: Moody, 2009.

Crawford, Matthew. *Shop Class as Soulcraft*. Reprint. London: Penguin, 2010.

Daniels, Denise, and Shannon Vandewarker. *Working in the Presence of God: Spiritual Practices for Everyday Work*. Peabody, MA: Hendrickson, 2019.

DeKoster, Lester. *Work: The Meaning of Your Life; A Christian Perspective*. Grand Rapids: Christian's Library Press, 1982.

Dik, Bryan J. *Redeeming Work: A Guide to Discovering God's Calling for Your Career*. West Conshohocken, PA: Templeton, 2020.

Doriani, Dan. *Work: Its Purpose, Dignity, and Transformation*. Phillipsburg, NJ: P&R, 2019.

Dyer, John. *From the Garden to the City: The Place of Technology in the Story of God*. 2nd ed. Grand Rapids: Kregel, 2022. Kindle.

Frankl, Viktor E. *Man's Search for Meaning*. Boston: Beacon, 1959. Kindle.

Garber, Steven. *Visions of Vocation: Common Grace for the Common Good*. Downers Grove, IL: InterVarsity, 2014.

Gill, David W. *Workplace Discipleship 101: A Primer*. Peabody, MA: Hendrickson, 2020.

Goossen, Richard J., and R. Paul Stevens. *Entrepreneurial Leadership: Finding Your Calling, Making a Difference*. Downers Grove, IL: InterVarsity, 2013.

Greene, Mark. Preface to *Transforming Vocation: Connecting Theology, Church, and the Workplace for a Flourishing World*, edited by David Benson et al., xiii–xxiii. Eugene, OR: Wipf & Stock, 2021.

Grudem, Wayne, and Barry Asmus. *The Poverty of Nations: A Sustainable Solution*. Wheaton: Crossway, 2013.

Guinness, Os. *The Call*. Nashville: Nelson, 2003.

Haanen, Jeff. *An Uncommon Guide to Retirement: Finding God's Purpose for the Next Season of Life*. Chicago: Moody, 2019.

Heatley, Bill. *The Gift of Work*. Colorado Springs: NavPress, 2008.

Hendricks, Bill. *The Person Called You: Why You're Here, Why You Matter and What You Should Do with Your Life*. Chicago: Moody, 2014.

Heschel, Abraham. *The Sabbath*. New York: Farrar, Straus & Giroux, 1951.

Hillman, Os. *The 9 to 5 Window: How Faith Can Transform the Workplace*. Ventura, CA: Regal Books, 2005.

Hull, Bill. *Christlike: The Pursuit of Uncomplicated Obedience*. Colorado Springs: NavPress, 2010.

Hunter, James. *To Change the World: The Irony, Tragedy, and Possibility of Christianity in the Late Modern World*. New York: Oxford University Press, 2010.

Issler, Klaus. *Living into the Life of Jesus*. Downers Grove, IL: InterVarsity, 2012.

Jensen, Phillip, and Tony Payne. *Beginnings: Eden and Beyond*. Faith and Walk Bible Studies. Wheaton: Crossway, 1999.

Kaemingk, Matthew, and Cory B. Wilson. *Work and Worship: Reconnecting Our Labor and Liturgy*. Grand Rapids: Baker Academic, 2020.

Kapic, Kelly. *You're Only Human: How Your Limits Reflect God's Design and Why That's Good News*. Grand Rapids: Brazos, 2022.

Keller, Timothy. *Every Good Endeavor: Connecting Your Work to God's Work*. New York: Riverhead, 2012.

———. *The Prodigal God: Recovering the Heart of the Christian Faith*. New York: Dutton, 2008.

Knapp, John C. *How the Church Fails Businesspeople (and What Can Be Done about It)*. Grand Rapids: Eerdmans, 2012.

Kreider, Alan. *The Patient Ferment of the Early Church: The Improbable Rise of Christianity in the Roman Empire*. Grand Rapids: Baker Academic, 2016.

Lewis, C. S. "Good Work and Good Works." In *The World's Last Night*. New York: Harcourt, Brace, 1952.

———. *Letters to Malcolm: Chiefly on Prayer*. San Diego: Harvest, 1964.

———. *The Lion, the Witch and the Wardrobe*. New York: HarperCollins, 1978.

———. *Miracles*. New York: HarperOne, 2001.

———. *The Weight of Glory*. New York: HarperOne, 2001.

Marshall, Paul, with Lela Gilbert. *Heaven Is Not My Home: Living in the Now of God's Creation*. Nashville: Word, 1998.

McDowell, Josh. *More Than a Carpenter*. Wheaton: Tyndale, 1977.

Meilaender, Gilbert. *The Freedom of a Christian: Grace, Vocation, and the Meaning of Our Humanity*. Grand Rapids: Brazos, 2006.

Miller, David. *God at Work: The History and Promise of the Faith and Work Movement*. New York: Oxford University Press, 2006.

Mouw, Richard. *He Shines in All That's Fair: Culture and Common Grace*. Grand Rapids: Eerdmans, 2002.

Nelson, Tom. *The Economics of Neighborly Love: Investing in Your Community's Compassion and Capacity*. Downers Grove, IL: InterVarsity, 2017.

———. *The Flourishing Pastor: Recovering the Lost Art of Shepherd Leadership*. Downers Grove, IL: InterVarsity, 2021.

———. *Work Matters: Connecting Sunday Worship to Monday Work*. Wheaton: Crossway, 2011.

Newbigin, Lesslie. *The Gospel in a Pluralist Society*. Grand Rapids: Eerdmans, 1989.

Nouwen, Henri. *In the Name of Jesus: Reflections on Christian Leadership*. Chestnut Ridge, PA: Crossroad Publishing Company, 1992.

O'Donnell, Michaela. *Make Work Matter: Your Guide to Meaningful Work in a Changing World*. Grand Rapids: Baker Books, 2021.

Placher, William C., ed. *Callings: Twenty Centuries of Christian Wisdom on Vocation*. Grand Rapids: Eerdmans, 2005.

Rae, Scott B. *Moral Choices: An Introduction to Ethics*. 4th ed. Grand Rapids: Zondervan, 2018.

Raynor, Jordan. *The Sacredness of Secular Work: Four Ways Your Job Matters for Eternity (Even When You're Not Sharing the Gospel)*. Colorado Springs: Waterbrook, 2024.

Sayers, Dorothy. "Why Work?," in *Leading Lives That Matter: What We Should Do and Who We Should Be*. Edited by Mark R. Schwehn and Dorothy C. Bass. Grand Rapids: Eerdmans, 2006.

Schwehn, Mark R., and Dorothy C. Bass, eds. *Leading Lives That Matter: What We Should Do and Who We Should Be.* Grand Rapids: Eerdmans, 2006.

Sherman, Amy L. *Agents of Flourishing: Pursuing Shalom in Every Corner of Society.* Downers Grove, IL: InterVarsity, 2022.

——. *Kingdom Calling: Vocational Stewardship for the Common Good.* Downers Grove, IL: InterVarsity, 2011.

Sinek, Simon. *Start with Why: How Great Leaders Inspire Everyone to Take Action.* New York: Penguin, 2009.

Smidt, Corwin. *Church State and Public Justice.* Downers Grove, IL: InterVarsity, 2007.

Sowell, Thomas. *Basic Economics: A Common Sense Guide to the Economy.* 4th ed. New York: Basic Books, 2010.

Stark, Rodney. *The Rise of Christianity: How the Obscure, Marginal Jesus Movement Became the Dominant Religious Force in the Western World in a Few Centuries.* Reprint. San Francisco: HarperSanFrancisco, 1997.

Stevens, R. Paul. *Aging Matters: Finding Your Calling for the Rest of Your Life.* Grand Rapids: Eerdmans, 2016.

——. *The Kingdom of God in Working Clothes: The Marketplace and Reign of God.* Eugene, OR: Wipf & Stock, 2022.

Stott, John. *Radical Disciple.* Downers Grove, IL: InterVarsity, 2010.

Suleyman, Mustafa. *The Coming Wave, Technology, Power and the Twenty-First Century's Greatest Dilemma.* New York: Crown, 2023.

Taylor, Charles. *A Secular Age.* Boston: Belknap, 2018.

Thompson, Curt. *The Anatomy of the Soul: Surprising Connections between Neuroscience and Spiritual Practices That Can Transform Your Life and Relationships.* Carol Stream, IL: Tyndale, 2010.

——. *The Soul of Shame: Retelling the Stories We Believe about Ourselves.* Downers Grove, IL: InterVarsity, 2015.

Thornton, Henry. *Devotional Prayers: With Scripture Memory Verses.* Chicago: Moody, 1993.

Trueman, Carl R. *The Rise and Triumph of the Modern Self: Cultural Amnesia, Expressive Individualism, and the Road to Sexual Revolution.* Wheaton: Crossway, 2020.

Veith, Gene. *God at Work: Your Christian Vocation in All of Life.* Wheaton: Crossway, 2002.

Volf, Miroslav. *Work in the Spirit: Toward a Theology of Work*. Eugene, OR: Wipf & Stock, 2001.

Warren, Tish Harrison. *Liturgy of the Ordinary: Sacred Practices in Everyday Life*. Downers Grove, IL: InterVarsity, 2016.

Willard, Dallas. *The Divine Conspiracy*. New York: HarperCollins, 1998.

——. *Hearing God*. Downers Grove, IL: InterVarsity, 1999.

——. *The Renovation of the Heart: Putting on the Character of Christ*. Colorado Springs: NavPress, 2002.

Willard, Dallas, and Gary Black Jr. *The Divine Conspiracy Continued: Fulfilling God's Kingdom on Earth*. New York: HarperCollins, 2014.

Williams, Paul S. *Exiles on Mission: How Christians Can Thrive in a Post-Christian World*. Grand Rapids: Brazos, 2020.

Wingren, Gustaf. *Luther on Vocation*. Translated by Carl C. Rasmussen. Evansville, IN: Ballast, 1994.

Wright, N. T. *Surprised by Hope: Rethinking Heaven, the Resurrection, and the Mission of the Church*. New York: Harper, 2008.

Zunker, Vernon. *Career, Work, and Mental Health: Integrating Career and Personal Counseling*. Thousand Oaks, CA: Sage, 2008.

Made
to Flourish

A call to all Christians
—

God wants us to worship him, to grow in discipleship, and to participate in his work in the world. This means that our faith is just as important on Monday as it is on Sunday.

Made to Flourish exists to close the gap between Sunday and Monday, to empower pastors and their churches to integrate faith, work, and economic wisdom — every day — for the flourishing of their communities. We create content, tools, and training designed to help Christians understand and embody what it looks like to live with no sphere of life untouched by God's plan to redeem the world and build his kingdom.

We want to help you integrate the Christian faith into all aspects of your professional and non-professional work. So go ahead and take the first step: Tell us about yourself at **madetoflourish.org/box**. When you do, we'll send you a box, filled (of course) with faith and work resources and an issue of our flagship magazine, *Common Good* — all for free, no strings attached.

Let's get to work.

MadetoFlourish.org